THE
LIFE AND LETTERS
OF
WALTER H. PAGE

Staff of the American Embassy in London, 1918

THE
LIFE AND LETTERS OF
WALTER H. PAGE

BY
BURTON J. HENDRICK

VOLUME III
PART II

GARDEN CITY   NEW YORK
DOUBLEDAY, PAGE & COMPANY
1926

CONTENTS

VOLUME III

PART II

THE
LIFE AND LETTERS
OF
WALTER H. PAGE

CHAPTER VIII

THE "DACIA" AND THE GERMAN-AMERICANS

I

THE story of the German merchantman *Dacia*—and Page's part in forestalling the crisis in British-American relations which it threatened—has already been told. This Presidential correspondence, however, gives the incident a new emphasis. The *Dacia* was one of the numerous German ships caught in American and other ports at the outbreak of the war. Great Britain's command of the sea kept all these vessels huddled in foreign harbours, but the war had hardly started when Congress passed a law that admitted foreign-built ships to American registry, an act that gave a great opportunity to German-Americans in the United States. A group headed by Mr. E. N. Breitung of Marquette, Michigan, purchased the *Dacia*, registered her as an American vessel, installed an American crew, raised the American flag, loaded the ship with cotton and prepared to sail for a German port. Would the British Navy seize the *Dacia* and confiscate it as enemy property? On the answer to this question might well depend peaceful relations between the United States and Great Britain. Page's dexterous suggestion that the French Navy stop the ship and take it to a prize court enabled the Allies to avoid this issue.

Americans at that time little understood the seriousness of the *Dacia* episode; there is practically nothing about it in Page's letters, the reason being that the discussion was carried on exclusively in cipher telegrams between the

London Embassy and the State Department. These telegrams, which are now available, bring home the fact that in the magnitude of the questions involved, the *Dacia* incident finds its historic parallel only in the *Trent* case of the Civil War. There were a few days in November, 1861, when it seemed impossible to avoid war between the United States and Great Britain. Peace was saved, indeed, only at the eleventh hour. Had another Ambassador than Page represented the United States in January, 1915, or had another man than Grey had charge of British foreign relations, the sailing of the *Dacia* might have had consequences of the most momentous character. Page himself describes his lengthy discussion with Sir Edward Grey on this subject as "the most ominous conversation I have ever had with him." The *Dacia* dispute was "ominous" because it involved several of the most critical issues of the war. On what side would the sympathies and possibly the support of the United States be thrown? What were the internal forces that really directed the official policy of this country? How formidable was the German-American population? Was it large enough and influential enough to control the action of the authorities at Washington? Above all the *Dacia* involved the great question of the use of British sea power. The most impressive feature of the European conflict was the complete control of the sea exercised by Great Britain. It had already become apparent that if the Allies were to win, or even to maintain the balanced situation that prevailed, they could do so only by the majestic omnipotence of the British fleet. Would Great Britain be permitted to use this naval strength in the way that under existing conditions it could most effectively be used? The German fleet declined to leave its ports and meet the naval power of Great Britain in battle, and the result was that the Allies could use their naval strength in only one way—that is, for the purpose of blockade. The United States was the only nation strong enough to oppose Great Britain in this programme, and the possible refusal of this country to recognize the blockade was a danger that constantly confronted the Allied cause.

Such a refusal would simply have meant that the Allies would have lost any chance they may have had of winning the war. Colonel Squier's recent visit to the Western Front had made this clear. He had brought to Page and to Washington the message—a message in which both General French and Lord Kitchener agreed—that the military situation was a hopeless deadlock. Against the apparently impregnable land forces of Germany, the Allies could hardly hope to make much progress; the only recourse left was that of starving the Central Empires to submission. A survey of the highways of commerce gave promise that this plan might succeed. The great foreign commerce which Germany had spent forty years in establishing had vanished, and the merchant fleet of the Fatherland was as useless as though it were lying at the bottom of the sea. The docks of New York were lined with vessels that had long been Germany's pride, while outside of New York Harbour lay several vigilant British cruisers instantly prepared to seize any one of them that stirred beyond the three-mile limit. Because this merchant marine was so inactive, the German population lacked food that would greatly have promoted its well-being, and the German Army lacked supplies that would have greatly increased its efficiency. At that time, in January, 1915, living conditions in Germany had not reached a serious stage, for the country had well prepared for a brief war; the time would come, however—as it ultimately did—when this isolation from world markets,

especially from the grain and cotton and copper of the
United States, would destroy the Central Empires. If
the German ships that were then marooned in American
harbours should again have free access to the seas Germany would have accomplished an important step in
abrogating the Allied blockade. Perhaps more ominous
still, if the United States released these German ships
for general commerce its action would have signified only
one thing, and that is that we had cast our support on
the side of Germany. We should at last have become
"unneutral," and unneutral in the interest of the Central
Empires.

These, therefore, were the great issues involved in the
Dacia. This is the reason why Grey regarded that vessel
as presenting the most "ominous" portent of the war.
The success of the German-Americans who had chartered
the ship would have meant the failure of Grey's diplomatic
efforts. His chief purpose, as already explained, had been
to conduct British foreign policy in a way that would
make the United States at least an economic support to
the Entente. Should the British fleet refrain from inter-
cepting the *Dacia*, or should that vessel once arrive at a
German or a Dutch port, Grey's policy would have gone
down in ruins. If German-Americans, or German sym-
pathizers, could purchase one German ship and restore
it to the sea, they could do the same thing with the great
German merchant fleet lying useless in American ports.
More important still such a success would have disclosed
that the German elements in this country had obtained a
determining influence on American policy, and this disclosure would have been almost as fatal to the Allied cause
as the breaking of their line in France. If they had obtained this preliminary victory, the Germans in this
country would have proceeded with other items of their

programme. The State Department had already taken the stand that the British attitude toward contraband was illegal, and it was well known that Washington would not recognize the blockade which the Allies intended soon to put in force. A victory in the *Dacia* episode would have given new inspiration to the German elements in the American population who were conducting a campaign against this blockade. It would also have encouraged them to add a new emphasis to another proposal which was now gaining considerable strength. At this time the prohibition of the shipment of American munitions to the Allies was an active question in Congress. Representative Richard Bartholdt, a man born in Germany, had introduced such a bill and was actively pushing it. It is therefore not surprising that Grey, in his talks with Page, constantly expressed his fear that German influence had gained the upper hand in the United States.

Above all, then, this was the apprehension that chiefly disturbed British statesmen. The restoration of German shipping to the seas would in itself have represented a calamity of great proportions; in the minds of the British leaders who were closely watching events in the United States the *Dacia* was important mainly as a portent—as the element in the situation which would determine whether the 6,000,000 or 7,000,000 Germans in the United States were sufficiently powerful, in a political sense, to control American policy in the interest of the Fatherland. In all Page's conversation with Grey this fear becomes the predominant note. "The talk about possible peace," Page telegraphs, "is very guarded and hesitating. Sir Edward Grey, who I think talks to me with unusual freedom, in a long unofficial conversation yesterday left the impression on my mind that until something definite came direct from Berlin there could be nothing worth discussing. There have been six 'offers' of peace, more or less vague, that have come indirectly to some one of the Allies, and these have not been frank or open. They were regarded either as dishonourable or as mere tricks to deceive the United States, unless it should be a direct open proposal. Sir Edward reminded me that whereas Englishmen in the United States become Americans many Germans in the United States remain Germans and carry on their struggle there against England. Hence the sale of passports recently unearthed to German subjects. Hence the trick played with the ship *Sacramento*. Hence Breitung's purchase of the *Dacia*. Hence Bartholdt's bill in Congress to forbid export of munitions. Hence many other acts by Germans in the United States that are part and parcel of Germany's war against England. He did not in the least imply any criticism of our government. But he made it perfectly clear that he regards the United States as one of the bases from which the Germans carry on the war in spite of our government's neutrality and in spite of the sympathy of most Americans for the Allies. They cannot buy arms there, but use the weapons of an organized propaganda in efforts to relieve England's economic pressure on Germany. These are reasons why anything that comes out of the United States arouses suspicion.

"The dangerous mood of public opinion about which I telegraphed you yesterday is largely caused by the British public's inability to make the distinction which Grey makes between the acts of our government and the acts of Germans in the United States. When they seem to coincide, as in the case of the *Sacramento* and the *Dacia*, British public opinion becomes inflammable. It continues to see what it regards as German influence in the prohibition for thirty days of ship manifests. I send you this as an effort to explain why the recently universally friendly public opinion here has become exceedingly suspicious and is fast becoming angry. People say that those Germans in America who are not Americans in fact even if some of them be so in form, are using their base of war in the United States in such ways as to nullify American neutrality. All this has so far had no open influence on this government but it is inevitable that it should have some effect on some members of the Government. When therefore General French was eager to know whether peace talk was merely a trick worked through the German war base in the United States he reflected the practically universal suspicion in and out of official life."

Telegram to Secretary of State

London, Jan. 15, 1915.

SECRETARY OF STATE,
    Washington.
        No. 1473

I read your instruction to Lord Haldane, who is in charge of Foreign Office during temporary absence of Sir Edward Grey, and discussed every phase of the subject.

He informed me that the Cabinet had already discussed it and reached a definite conclusion as follows: The Government has no wish to obstruct the cotton trade and is aware of its importance to the producers and to the United States. If, therefore, the *Dacia* come loaded with cotton, whether bound for Rotterdam or for Bremen, the British Government would see to it that the owners of the cotton should lose nothing. The Government will buy it, paying the price which had been arranged by contract with the German buyers.

But under international law and usage, His Majesty's

Government felt bound to refer to the public refusals by the purchase and the dispatch of this ship on such an errand. The ship, therefore, will be put into the Prize Court if she come.

Lord Haldane said further that if the *Dacia* were used under bona fide American register in coast-wise trade, or in trade with South America, his government would not object. I asked him if this remark would apply to other German ships now interned in the United States and he replied "yes."

AMERICAN AMBASSADOR,
London.

Telegram to President and Secretary

London, January 18, 1915.

SECRETARY OF STATE,
    Washington.

For Secretary and the President.   Strictly confidential. Very confidential.

I have had more than an hour's talk with Sir Edward Grey. He confirms what Haldane told me about the *Dacia*, but he does not confirm what Haldane said about other German ships in the last sentence of my 1473, January fifteenth. About this they are not agreed and the Cabinet will have further discussion. It will be prudent to disregard the last sentence above referred to. Apparently Haldane went beyond what had been agreed on by the Cabinet. My inquiry whether the British Government would object to the purchase and transfer of German-interned ships to ply between American and British ports brought from Sir Edward Grey the most ominous conversation I have ever had with him.

He explained that the chief weapon that England has against any enemy is her navy and that the navy may

damage an enemy in two ways: by fighting and by economic pressure. Under the conditions of this war economic
pressure is at least as important as naval fighting. One
of the chief methods of using economic pressure is to force
the German merchant ships off the seas. If, therefore,
these be bought and transferred to a neutral flag this
pressure is removed.

He reminded me that he was not making official repre-
sentations to the United States Government, and for that
reason he was the more emphatic. If the United States,
without intent to do Great Britain an injury but moved
only to relieve the scarcity of tonnage, should buy these
ships, it would still annul one of the victories that England has won by her navy. He reminded me of the fast-
rising tide of criticism of the United States about the
transfer of the *Dacia*, and he declared that this has in-
tensified and spread the feeling against us in England on
account of our note of protest. He spoke earnestly,
sadly, ominously, but in the friendliest spirit.

The foregoing only confirms the following paragraphs
which I wrote yesterday and held till I could see Grey
to-day. There is a steadily deepening and spreading
feeling throughout every section of English opinion that
the German influence in the United States has by this
temptation to buy these interned ships won us to the
German side. The old criticism of the President for not
protesting against the violation of the Hague Treaty by
Germany when she invaded Belgium is revived with ten-
fold its first earnestness. This is coupled with our protest
against shipping as showing an unfriendly spirit. But
both these criticisms were relatively mild till the *Dacia*
was transferred to the American flag. That transfer
added volume and vehemence to all preceding criticisms
and is cited in the press and in conversation everywhere

as proof of our unfriendliness. They regard the *Dacia* as a German ship put out of commission by their navy. She comes on the seas again by our permission which so far nullifies their victory. If she come here she will, of course, be seized and put into the Prize Court. Her seizure will strike the English imagination in effect as the second conquest of her, first from the Germans and now from the Americans. Popular feeling will, I fear, run as high as it ran over the *Trent* affair; and a very large part of English opinion will regard us as enemies.

If another German ship should follow the *Dacia* here I do not think that any government could withstand the popular demand for her confiscation; and if we permit the transfer of a number of these ships there will be such a wave of displeasure as will make a return of the recent good feeling between the two peoples impossible for a generation. There is no possible escape from such an act being regarded by the public opinion of this Kingdom as a distinctly unfriendly and practically hostile act.

I not only read and hear this at every turn—I feel it in the attitude of people toward me and toward our government. For the first time I have felt a distinctly unfriendly atmosphere. It has the quality of the atmosphere just before an earthquake.

The Government is studiously polite and still genuinely friendly. But there are warnings that it may not be able to maintain its old-time friendly attitude if a whirl-wind of anti-American feeling sweep over the kingdom and over its Allies. Nine men out of every ten you meet in London to-day are convinced that the *Dacia* is proof that the Germans have won us to their support. I cannot exaggerate the ominousness of the situation. The case is not technical but has large human and patriotic and historic elements in it.

AMERICAN AMBASSADOR,
London.

II

How much reason was there for this British fear of German-American influence with the Washington Administration? In the British Cabinet there were plenty of practical politicians who, unfamiliar as they might be with all the complexities of American affairs, readily understood the power that a compact bloc of voters might wield in the counsels of a political party dependent upon popular support for its continuance in office. In Britain itself they knew that considerations like these might be regarded in the formation of public policies, and it seemed hardly likely that so expert a manipulator of political groups as Mr. Bryan, to say nothing of President Wilson himself, would ignore so demonstrative a minority as the German-Americans. The *Dacia* telegrams brought an answer directly from the President himself, an answer that has an interest that extends far beyond the *Dacia* episode. In this communication President Wilson outlined the ideas that underlay his policy in the prevailing controversies. He yielded nothing on the legal issues involved in the pending dispute. The American Government still maintained its position that the transfer of a German-built, German-owned ship to American registry did not violate international law, and placed the responsibility for her seizure upon the nation that should take this step. The President, that is, endorsed the position of Mr. Breitung and his associates, who had recently purchased the vessel, and again took issue with the British Foreign Office in the matter of the blockade. This message therefore left the two countries deadlocked as before.

Even more important, however, was President Wilson's rejoinder to the apprehension, evidently deeply lodged in the mind of Sir Edward Grey, that the German-American elements in the United States were exerting almost a decisive influence on American war policy. He even took the trouble to set the British mind right on the question of the racial constituents of the American population. Page was instructed to correct the opinion evidently prevalent in Great Britain that the United States was predominantly British in its racial composition. If the British believed that American sympathy should naturally incline to the Allies because Americans were themselves largely of British stock, such a belief, judging from the President's words, rested upon an unwarranted assumption. President Wilson's analysis was incomplete, yet his sentences did contain the implication, perhaps because of this very incompleteness, that the British elements in the United States were no longer numerically important. On the other hand the President placed emphasis upon the German and Irish contributions to the American composite. One might reasonably assume from the President's statement of the case that the British peoples formed at present merely one constituent in an extremely varied whole and that other races, especially the German, were more numerous. President Wilson was an eminent historian and would probably have denied that this interpretation was justified. Had Sir Edward Grey ever read his dispatch, however, he would not have been far wrong had he concluded that the several races in the United States exercised a certain influence upon American foreign policy, that the British stock was not large, and that German-Americans in particular were sufficiently numerous to make their voices heard in the councils of the Department of State.

"The President," Mr. Bryan telegraphed, "directs me to send the following: 'Answering your two telegrams in regard to the irritation and apparent change in public opinion regarding the United States you will please discuss the matter again with Sir Edward Grey in effect as follows: We regret exceedingly to learn that the British public entertains any doubt as to the strict neutrality of this Government or as to the support given by the general public to the Government's position. This is probably due to the fact that a portion of the British public is quite naturally uninformed as to the character of our population. While the English element predominated in the original stock the immigration in latter years has been largely from other countries. Germany and Ireland, for instance, have contributed very materially during the last half century, and among those who are the children of foreign-born parents the German element now predominates. This element is not only numerous but it has a strong representation in financial, mercantile life and agriculture. . . . There is, of course, not the slightest alteration in the cordial feeling which has always existed between the United States and Great Britain. Mere debate and newspaper agitation will not alter that feeling; but acts which seem to them arbitrary, unnecessary, and contrary to the recognized rules of neutral commerce may alter it very seriously, because the great majority of our people are trying in good faith to live within those rules, and they are sensitive about nothing more than about their legitimate trade. . . . The export of arms, ammunition, and horses to the Allies is, of course, known, and the protest made by German-Americans and by a portion of the Irish-Americans, while entirely without justification, is not unnatural. It is difficult for people to think logically when their sympathies are aroused. The Government has done all in its power to make the situation plain and has to-day issued a lengthy letter answering numerous criticisms that have been made. . . . '"

Whether a great nation should guide itself even to a slight extent by the aspirations and prejudices of the different races that form its population, is a question that may be argued; it should be pointed out, however, that the President's description of the American composite, or at least the inference that may be drawn from his somewhat careless treatment of the subject, is inaccurate. The fact is that the British elements in the United States at the present time are enormously greater than those of any other people. The question was thoroughly investigated by the census bureau in 1910[1] and its report on this subject is available to any interested student. The belief that the United States is a racial conglomerate, with no one outstanding population upon which the nation rests as a secure foundation; that, in other words, there are no "Americans," is one of the most prevailing misconceptions of the day. The census report in question shows that the white population of the United States in 1790 was 3,200,000, and that practically all of this was of British and principally of English origin. This stock was extremely prolific for the first sixty years of the Republic, so prolific, indeed, that by 1910, this original population had increased to 39,000,000. In the last hundred years the immigration from England, Scotland, and Wales, as well as from the British provinces in Canada, has been much greater than is popularly believed. The official conclusion is that, of the 94,000,000 white men, women,

---

[1] See "A Century of Population Growth in the United States," published by the United States Census Bureau.

and children, living in the United States in 1910, about
55,000,000 traced their origin to England, Scotland, and
Wales. This, then, is approximately the British contribu-
tion to the American population. The race that ranks next
to the British is the German, who numbered, according
to the census of 1910, 8,200,000, and next to this the Irish,
4,500,000. It is an almost startling fact that this native
American population forms the largest body of Anglo-
Saxons in the world. It is larger than the combined
population of Great Britain, Canada, Australia, and New
Zealand. Compared with it the other stocks in the United
States are exceedingly small. It is quite apparent therefore that President Wilson's discussion of the subject,
if not inaccurate, or misleading, was certainly incomplete.

Page asked permission to withhold this dispatch for
the time being and present its contents to Sir Edward
Grey "when a favourable opportunity occurs." It may
safely be assumed that this "favourable opportunity"
never came. In this struggle, as ultimately in all others,
the German-Americans failed. The Administration did
not waver in its attitude, and the *Dacia*, loaded with cotton, sailed for a European port. Page, as related in a
previous volume, had dropped a hint to the British that
its seizure by a French vessel would probably not cause a
"diplomatic incident." The points involved were precisely the same, but the "atmosphere" would be quite
different. Sentiment was still a strong emotion with
Americans; memories of the Revolution were keen,
and the traditional American friendship for France an
active force; thus it would be impossible to rouse the
popular mind against "depredations" committed by the
French Navy. Page's advice was followed; as soon as
the *Dacia* appeared in the British Channel a French

cruiser seized her, took her into a French harbour, and put
her in a French prize court. Thus ended the great
German-American plan to restore the interned German
merchant vessels to the seas. No more *Dacias* sailed
from American ports, and the great German merchant
fleet interned in the United States remained there until
the American Government, on its own declaration of war,
itself took possession of the German ships. By a threat
of resignation, Page had persuaded Washington to back
down on the Declaration of London, and now, by a quiet
hint dropped to Sir Edward Grey, he had prevented the
Dacia crisis from becoming what the *Trent* crisis almost
became in 1861—the cause of war between the United
States and Great Britain—with consequences to the future
of mankind too appalling to contemplate.

CHAPTER IX

THE "LUSITANIA"

I

THE *Lusitania* was torpedoed May 7, 1915. Page's experiences during that period have already been described, and the letters written both to the President and Colonel House have been printed.[1] Several telegrams sent the President and the Secretary of State, however, add emphasis to his views. The following message, dated May 8th, the day after the *Lusitania* disaster, is the earliest official paper dealing with the great issues raised by this calamity. In it Page reports the British and the European view that the United States, by declaring war at that time, could quickly bring the conflict to an end.

Telegram to the President

London, May 8 [1915], 5 P. M.

Confidential in the extreme. For the President and the Secretary only. As nearly as I can interpret public opinion here as affected by the sinking of the *Lusitania*, it is as follows, which I transmit for your information:

A profound effect has been produced on English opinion in general regarding both the surprising efficiency of the German submarine work and the extreme recklessness of the Germans. The sinking of the *Lusitania*, following the use of poisonous gas and the poisoning of wells and the torpedoing of the *Gulflight* and other plainly marked

[1] Volume II, Chapter XV.

neutral ships, the English regard as the complete abandonment of war regulations and of humanity in its conduct, as well as of any consideration for neutrals. Sir Edward Grey said to me last night, "They are running amuck." It is war under the black flag. Indignation in the aggregate reached a new pitch.

Official comment is of course reticent. The freely expressed unofficial feeling is that the United States must declare war or forfeit European respect. So far as I know this opinion is universal. If the United States come in, the moral and physical effect will be to bring peace quickly and to give the United States a great influence in ending the war and in so reorganizing the world as to prevent its recurrence. If the United States submit to German disregard of her citizens' lives and of her property and of her neutral rights on the sea, the United States will have no voice or influence in settling the war or in what follows for a long time to come. This, so far as I can ascertain, is the practically unanimous opinion here. The Americans in London are outspoken to the same effect.

Much the profoundest depression is felt to-day that has been felt since the war began and British opinion is stirred to its depths.

The foreign editor of the *Times*,[1] a usually well-informed and trustworthy man, who knows all the principal European statesmen, is just returned from a week in France. He tells me in strictest confidence that England, France, and Russia made a bargain with Italy on April 30th, agreeing to cede to Italy very large parts of Austrian territory some of which has a Slavic population, if Italy come into the war within a month. This was done without consulting Serbia and against her wishes. Italy will soon come in if she keep her agreement, to be followed

[1] H. Wickham Steed.

by Rumania. I have heard unofficial confirmation of this agreement here.

The same editor informs me that General Joffre told him that he is confident that he would break through the German lines within a month.

I have heard the opinion expressed to-day in several well-informed but unofficial quarters that warlike action by the United States would be a signal for other neutral nations whose rights Germany has disregarded, especially the Scandinavian countries and possibly Holland. For the correctness of this view I cannot vouch but I know it is widely entertained.

AMERICAN AMBASSADOR,
London.

The sequel made it sufficiently plain that any policy remotely resembling this was not contemplated by the White House. That the suggestion was unwelcome appears from a brief letter written by the President to Mr. Bryan who was then—and for a short time afterward —Secretary of State. In the archives of the State Department President Wilson's letter is attached to the original copy of Page's historic telegram. This small sheet of paper pictures one of the most critical moments in the war. Page's message was received less than twenty-four hours after the *Lusitania* had gone down with the loss of more than one hundred American lives. It reached the White House late at night. At that moment President Wilson was the one man above all others in whose hands the future of America and Europe lay. Every mind and every heart in two continents were centred upon that solitary figure in the White House. Popular emotion in the United States had seldom reached the intensity that then stirred nearly a hundred million Americans.

Whatever differences of opinion and sentiment may have appeared in the nearly two years of discussion that ensued, there is not the slightest doubt that Americans, or the vast majority of them, sympathized at that moment with the views set forth in Page's telegram. That Mr. Wilson kept himself carefully secluded from popular emotions for the few days following the *Lusitania* is well known. He saw no members of his Cabinet, not even the member whose department was chiefly concerned with that event. For several days Mr. Bryan held himself in readiness for the Presidential call, but Mr. Wilson never summoned him. So far as is known, Mr. Wilson's only communication with his Secretary of State, preceding the Cabinet meeting of Tuesday, May 12th, was the extremely brief but enlightening note written concerning Page's urgent telegram, printed above. The letter was typewritten, evidently by the President's own hand, for the type has the familiar character of the Hammond machine, on which the President typed his own messages and confidential documents.

It appears at once that Page's presentation of the *Lusitania* case fell upon unsympathetic ears. The President's comment is dated May 10th, which was the Sunday after the sinking had taken place. It was on the evening of the same day that the President went to Philadelphia and delivered the speech in which were embedded the celebrated words, "There is such a thing as a nation being too proud to fight." The letter to Mr. Bryan, which must have been the only light he obtained upon the President's views before the first *Lusitania* note was handed to him for signature and which, as a matter of fact, is probably the only evidence existing of the state of the presidential mind at this crisis, is as follows:

The President to the Secretary of State

The White House, Washington,
10 May, 1915.

MY DEAR MR. SECRETARY:

After all, this* does not express Page's own opinion, but what he takes to be public opinion at the moment in Great Britain.

It is a very serious thing to have such things thought, because everything that affects the opinion of the world regarding us affects our influence for good.

Faithfully yours,
W. W.

*Page's dispatch about the *Lusitania* which I find I have burned.

The next day Page again became urgent:

Telegram to the President

London, May 11, 1915.

2080, May 11, 1 P. M.

Confidential.   To the Secretary and the President.

Continuing my report of British feeling and opinion. Every day without news of definite action by the American Government about the *Gulflight* and the *Lusitania* deepens the British suspicion into a conviction that our government will content itself with mere argumentative protests. The respectful and sympathetic silence of the first few days' excitement is now giving way to open criticism of American failure to realize the situation and of American unwillingness to act.   There is a good deal of contempt in British feeling.   This contempt is not based upon British wish for military help, but on the feeling that America falls short morally to condemn German methods and has fallen victim to German propaganda and does not properly rate German character as shown in war nor understand German danger to all free institutions. Fear grows of a moral failure on the part of the United States.

The most conservative action hoped for by the best friends of America here is that diplomatic relations be severed with Germany pending satisfactory settlement and that Congress be convened so that the voice of the nation may be heard.

The aristocratic element of English life, which enjoys social and governmental privileges and is what we should call reactionary, consciously or unconsciously hopes for American inactivity to justify their distrust of democratic institutions. Their feeling is that Great Britain will emerge from the war far more powerful than ever and they are content that the United States should be of as slight influence in the world as possible. The few expressions that the United States will remain neutral and will refrain from breaking off diplomatic relations with Germany come from this element of English society and unofficially from governing circles.

Official life here is studiously silent to me. The few persons who have called to express condolence or who have written letters of sympathy about the *Lusitania* are all, I think, more or less close personal friends who feel free to speak for personal reasons.

The impression is clear that delay in definite action in some really effective form or failure to act definitely will shut the United States out of British and I should guess of all European respect for a generation.

AMERICAN AMBASSADOR,
London.

Telegram to the President

London, May 12, 1915.

2091, May 12, 5 P. M.

Confidential.   To the Secretary and the President.

A memorial service for the *Lusitania* victims, including American victims, is being arranged in St. Paul's.   I have insisted there shall be no sermon or discourse.

The feeling among Americans in London, residents and visitors, increases.   More than one group has prepared resolutions critical of what they regard as our government's delay.   I am encouraging Hoover and others in the efforts they are making to prevent a mass meeting of Americans which I hope will be successful.

AMERICAN AMBASSADOR,
London.

President Wilson's first *Lusitania* note gave Page great satisfaction.   In it the President severely arraigned Germany and virtually demanded that she abandon unrestricted submarine warfare, disavow the *Lusitania* sinking and pay an indemnity.   The alternative—such was the interpretation generally given this note in the United States and in Europe—was war with this country.   "The Imperial German Government," said Mr. Wilson, "will not expect the Government of the United States to omit any word or any act necessary to the performance of its sacred duty of maintaining the rights of the United States and its citizens, and of safeguarding their free exercise and enjoyment."   Such was the concluding sentence of the first *Lusitania* note and it was accepted as definitely committing the United States to vigorous action.   In itself it sufficiently accounts for the tone of Page's next message.

Telegram to the President

London, May 16, 1915.

2104, May 16, 10 P. M.

Commendation of the note to Germany and gratification are universally expressed privately and in the press. The *Times* says: "It is a note that both in substance and expression recalls the best traditions of American diplomacy. The stand taken by President Wilson is something more than a declaration of national policy. Nothing less than the conscience of humanity makes itself audible in his measured and incisive sentences." The *Times* editorial ends in these words: "The moral interests of the United States and the Allies are henceforward indissolubly linked."

The *Westminster Gazette* says: "We count this note as from all human and moral points of view the greatest event of this war."

(*Cipher*) The following is in the Secretary's private code and confidential to the President and the Secretary. Among the men whose private expressions of praise have come to me are most members of the Government as well as Lansdowne, Balfour, and Bonar Law, of the opposition.

I think the practically unanimous expectation here is that the German Government will give an evasive answer and decline to abbreviate the use of submarines against merchant ships.

The representatives of other neutral governments here privately express pleasure and gratitude. The Americans in London about whose impatience I telegraphed feel ashamed of their hasty fears.

May I be allowed to express my personal congratulations on the note?

AMERICAN AMBASSADOR,
London.

However, this satisfaction was short lived. Germany's absurd answer to this first *Lusitania* note, in which she practically ignored the points insisted on by President Wilson, and defended her action on the ground that the torpedoed vessel was a warship, itself armed with guns and carrying munitions and troops to Great Britain; her refusal to accept the President's demands; the Kaiser's policy of evasion and delay; and the President's failure to follow his imperious words with acts, produced that doubt in Page's mind and, afterward, that complete divergence of views and sympathy, that now become the prevailing tone in the Ambassador's communications. Mr. Lansing's succession to the State Department after Mr. Bryan's resignation did little to improve British-American relations. From the beginning of the war, indeed, Mr. Lansing, as Counsellor of the Department, had formulated and directed American policy in the blockade. Now that he had become Secretary of State, Mr. Lansing insisted, more energetically than ever, that this blockade was illegal, and it is perhaps not strange that the feeling became broadcast that if the American Government were not anti-British it was at least not especially sympathetic to the cause of the Allies. As the summer wore on, the fear in Washington that the German submarine campaign would result in a crisis between the United States and Germany becomes more apparent. Any step that would ruffle German sensibilities was carefully avoided. Word came to Page—or at least Page so interpreted an indirect message—that it might be well for him to go to the United States for a face-to-face discussion. He intimated a willingness, even an eagerness to do so. President Wilson, however, abruptly vetoed the plan. "He thinks," telegraphed Mr. Lansing, "that it would be very unwise for you to come at this time, since it would create an impression that something unusually critical and of a most confidential nature had arisen which could not be handled by correspondence." Even trifles revealed the sensitiveness of Washington on the subject of German relations:

To the Secretary of State

London, June 22, 1915.

2329, June 22.

John S. Sargent, the distinguished American artist resident in London, has a decoration conferred several years ago by the German Emperor, which he now wishes to return. He has handed me a note addressed to the proper Court authority in Berlin respectfully returning the decoration, and he asks me if he may send it to you under cover of a letter, requesting you to ask Gerard to deliver it in Berlin or if I under your instructions may send it to Gerard direct.

The return of such honours has become quite common between Englishmen and Germans.

He asks me also if I may transmit through Gerard his resignation from two notable art societies in Berlin and Munich.

Sargent makes no criticism of German Government or German societies in his letters but merely resigned because he is no longer in sympathy with German aims. I await instructions.

AMERICAN AMBASSADOR,
London.

From the Secretary of State

Washington, June 23, 1915.

Your 2329, June 22.

Not matters with which Department or its officers abroad can have any connection.

Sargent should reimburse Embassy for your telegram and pay for this reply, five dollars.

LANSING.

To the President

London, July 15, 1915.

2462, July 15, 11 A. M.

Confidential.   For the President and the Secretary.

I interpret thoughtful and responsible opinion here as follows and send it as in the past for your information. Germany reckons on American unpreparedness for war and hopes that pro-German sentiment can prevent munitions from going to the Allies, arguing that, if pro-German sentiment fail, the United States cannot fight and therefore the risk of insulting us is negligible, since, as a neutral, her enemies obtain help from us through their command of the seas, and as an enemy we could do no more harm than we now do.

The feeling seems to be that Germany can never be permitted to give us a satisfactory answer, and that if we do not take effective action of some sort we shall lose the confidence and respect of the Allies and in time have to face Germany alone; that if democracy as represented by the United States yield, its standing in the world will be gone for an indefinite time and its advocates weakened in every country.

Men here point out the similarity of Germany's dealing with the United States to her dealing with England, always by evasion, and they point to England's mistake in hoping to avoid war and not equipping an army ten years ago.   They say that unless German military power is crushed by the crushing of the professional military party, all the world will be terrorized, and that we must range out effectively against this menace without delay or suffer ultimately whatever the outcome of the present struggle may be.

I think this opinion is practically universal here among thoughtful men. They are saddened by it but regard it as practically certain that we cannot escape; that the Germans will continue assassination and incendiarism in the United States and will sooner or later destroy more American travellers.

British opinion has great and growing confidence in the President himself but seems to show a doubt about the virility and courage of American public opinion, attributing to it a timidity arising from failure to grasp the scope of the issues involved in the struggle and the effect of its outcome on the United States.

AMERICAN AMBASSADOR,
London.

Telegram to the President

London, August 24, 1915.
Confidential for the Secretary and the President.

I report the following as indicating public opinion here for whatever it may be worth, if it be worth anything.

Sir William Mather,[1] who, you know, is a good representative of conservative-minded, non-political, thoughtful Englishmen, called to see me yesterday to express the friendly grave fear lest delay in action should deepen the impression throughout Europe that the United States is seeking to maintain peace at the price of humiliat on in the face of repeated offences. This fear is becoming more or less general, even among thoughtful men.

The reported intention of our government, published here, to give Germany another opportunity to explain

[1] Of Manchester; a prominent Liberal and one of the leaders in education in Great Britain.

and thereby to evade and to cause delay provokes the general opinion that any delayed action on our part will lose much of its moral effect by tardiness.

The tone of the less responsible press is a tone of open ridicule. The tone of the best papers shows surprise at what they regard as an unfortunate delay and a restrained fear lest the United States delay too long.

Several men in official life have expressed opinions such as the opinion that follows. They have spoken, not to me but in quarters where they knew I should hear it: "The Germans shuffled and evaded and lied to us for ten years and we refused to believe that this was their deliberate policy. The Americans seem slow to learn by our experience. They have a contempt for the United States as they had for England and they hope to keep her writing letters at which they laugh."

The facts about the *Arabic*[1] seem so clear here as to leave no doubt of her deliberate sinking by the German submarine without any protection. The testimony of all survivors is identical on all important particulars.

AMERICAN AMBASSADOR,
London.

Telegram to the President

London, September 8, 1915.

Strictly confidential. For the Secretary and the President only.

The feeling even of conservative men here seems hardening into the conviction that the United States is losing the fear and therefore the respect of foreign governments and of foreign opinion. The sinking of the *Arabic* and the apparent acceptance of Bernstorff's assurance of the cessation of submarine attacks on passenger ships created

[1]Torpedoed August 19, 1915.

a bad impression because the assurance was not frank and specific and because no mention was made of the *Lusitania*. Fear of the same acquiescence in the torpedoing of the *Hesperian* is provoking ridicule and is fortifying the belief that we will desist from action under any provocation. This feeling is not confined to those who would like to have us enter the war, but it exists among our best friends, who think we ought to keep out of actual war. They seem to construe our attitude as proof of weakness and there is danger that whatever we may say hereafter will be listened to with less respect. I think I detect evidence already of a diminishing respect for our communications. The impression grows that the "peace at any price" type of man has control of American opinion. Dumba's remaining would certainly tend to deepen this feeling into a permanent conviction.

You must read this not as my opinion but as my interpretation of responsible opinion here. Men here are of course likely to form judgments on partial selfishness, but I have tried to leave out of account the ordinary temporary selfish section of public opinion and to include only that which looks as if it may become the permanent English judgment of the American democracy. Thinking men persist in regarding the United States as a more or less loose aggregation of different nationalities, without national unity, national aims, or definite moral qualities.

AMERICAN AMBASSADOR,
London.

To the President

London, August 19, 1915.

DEAR MR. PRESIDENT:

As this amazing tragedy unfolds itself we know only imperfectly what is happening and we can only guess what is going to happen.   But from what I hear and can infer we had as well prepare our minds and our plans for a long war yet.   If the Allies make a peace that leaves the Germans really victorious, they'll have to fight again, perhaps with fewer of them united than now.   They'd rather suffer extinction now than later, and they'll not quit till they are obliged to quit or till they win.   I hear that neither side can win in France.   The report (private) here is that a little while ago the French, with half-a-million men, tried to break through the German line, that they advanced about five miles and had lost more than two hundred thousand, and that they then gave it up.   It is said also that the Germans have no expectation of breaking through in France.   If these reports be true and for the present at least they seem true, the land-war will be decided in Turkey, in the Balkans, or in Russia, tho' Russian defeat alone can decide nothing.   This seems to mean a long struggle—through the winter and nobody knows how much longer.   England is alive to the peril, and she'll spend her last shilling and (eventually) send her last man. She regards English civilization as at stake.   And England is so slow that she'll not marshall all her strength till the other Allies are exhausted.   No end, therefore, seems in sight.

But following this war, as there followed all preceding great wars, will be great changes in the rules of the game as between belligerents.   Men used to say that the machines of destruction would become so terrible as to make war impossible, for it would mean mere extermination. The war in France is already that—the only question is, which side will be exterminated?   The trench, the machine-gun, the hand-mortar, the hand-grenade, and gas (yet in its experimental stage) are killing men in such numbers that neither the French nor the Germans report the facts—to say nothing of explosive shells from howitzers. Several British regiments now contain hardly a man—private or officer—who first went out. The gentle euphemism for this annihilation is "wastage." Fighting above ground is obsolete where both sides are "scientific." And annihilation is going on in France as fast as any theorist could wish. Of course it takes time to annihilate millions of men: the army unit has increased so enormously. And the population of parts of Poland is suffering annihilation, as a part of the population of northern France and of Belgium did. Starvation and the use of gas will become conventionalized in future wars, whether "legalized" or not. In fact, they are already accepted weapons in this war. The mistake made by those who predicted that the horrors of war with new engines would make wars impossible was not a mistake about annihilation but about the shrinking of men from being annihilated. No such fear stops them. In fact it looks as if war now means practical extermination. If the Belgians ever get into Germany or the Germans ever get into England or Italy, something very closely akin to extermination will follow. Men were once horrified by the use of the cross-bow in war, and by the use of guns—all the old rules of sword and pike war were knocked out by these dishonourable new weapons of indiscriminate destruction. So the art of killing moves on towards a gas that will annihilate an army or devastate a province.

As for our controversy with Great Britain, this seems to me as good a forecast as can now be made: The blockade, as defended by Sir Edward Grey, rests on his citations of American action during the Civil War and on his willingness, if need be, to submit disputes to arbitration. Unless some influence that I do not now foresee comes in to play a part, this government will stand on that con-tention. They will conduct the blockade as favourably to us as they can bring themselves to do; but they are per-suaded, perhaps over-persuaded, that the economic pressure on Germany is their strongest weapon. Public opinion here takes that view more and more decisively, and members of both parties that form the Coalition Government have committed themselves to this belief. Since they are willing to submit their action to arbi-tration—taking the risk of another *Alabama* award—they hope to get through on this basis. I think we did a good stroke in drawing from Sir Edward Grey his note declaring his willingness to submit to arbitration. This seems to me our real triumph so far in the controversy.

The trouble that the controversy gives you they follow and share. They know the Hoke Smiths[1] and the other agitators and they have their share of alarm. But (I think) they are going to keep up their economic pressure on Germany at all hazards. The public will rend the Government if it does not.

Yet thoughtful men here know that Great Britain will come out of this war at the best with great financial and commercial embarrassment, and at the worst practically bankrupt along with all the other European governments; and they know that the United States will have a prodi-gious advantage over any other country for a generation or two, which (barring some great misfortune to us) will mean a prodigious advantage for all time. They wish, therefore, to stand close to us, for selfish reasons, reasons of self-preservation, as well as for reasons of civilization—the preservation of Anglo-Saxon insti-tutions and aspirations. If we get through this war amicably with the British, they will be more friendly

[1]Senator from Georgia and a vigorous protestant against the British blockade.

to us[1] than they have ever been, since we have not only the largest English-speaking white population but will have the start also definitely towards financial and commercial supremacy. Their predominant financial grip on the world, which is their main grip, will be gone. And, tho' they have not lost their virility, they have never acquired our efficiency. They are slow and unadaptable and tradition-ridden and class-ridden yet. On any street-corner in London you have to buy one afternoon paper from one man, another from another and a third from a third. It has never occurred to any one man to sell two or more papers. I passed two men the other day in the country each trying to coax a horse hitched to a great load of hay up a steep hill. Each horse had more than it could pull. I said, "Why don't you hitch both horses to one cart, pull that up and then come back and get the other cart in the same way?" After a moment of surprised silence and deep thought, one of them answered, "We've never done that, sir," and he went on urging his horse up inch by inch. That night at a country hotel, lighted by electricity, they charged me for candles.

"But I had no candles."

"Yes, sir, but we've always done that."

These little experiences explain the lack of munitions six months after the munition works had been begging for orders. They explain the effort to take the Dardanelles without an army. They explain the postponement of conscription, although everybody knows that England will have to put her last available man in the army. The amazing thing is, the men who sell only one paper each continue to sell them, the men with the carts do get up the

---

[1] I should say more dependent on us, rather than more friendly to us. (W. H. P.'s note.)

hill, the hotel landlady got my money for candles, the Government is getting munitions at last, and the Dardanelles will be taken even if all Egypt has become a vast hospital for English needlessly wounded. In none of these activities, however, has the Englishman had the direct competition of the Yankee. When he encounters that, good-bye, John. And that's what he will encounter when the war ends and leaves him poor.

He understands that his financial primacy is in danger and he will do his utmost to keep close to us.

There come dull and depressing ruts in this road that we now travel, and we are now in such a rut. Everybody who can leave London is gone. Most houses where one meets people who know things or who think they know are closed. Even the clubs are deserted. Members of the Government themselves—as many as can—try to find seclusion and a little rest in the country a few days in the week. Most of the diplomatic corps have gone to the country and come into town for office hours every day— an utter delusion unless they have babies in the family; and the only diplomatic family here that has babies is the Chinaman's. My house is as good a place as there is in England for me as long as this nightmare lasts—except, of course, every normal man hates a town. But this isn't a bad summer town. It isn't really hot, as you know; and there are golf links within fifteen minutes of my office. House be hanged! His kind solicitude for me is a case of benevolence badly wasted. But it is a dull and depressing period. The streets and parks are full of wounded soldiers. So is all England, for that matter. I saw them in every village I drove through in the Midlands last Saturday and Sunday. The price of good food goes higher and higher. Women make the hay in the fields, punch your ticket at the railway stations, and take your fare in the street cars in some cities. My shoemaker sent only yesterday a pair of shoes that I ordered nearly three months ago: "My men have gone to the war." The up-town part of the city is nearly deserted. Shops and residences are to let on almost every street. The newspapers have little but Russian defeats and assaults by Hoke Smith—two curious sources of sorrow! Poor old John Bull, he pathetically looks to the United States for sympathy, and he's "muddling through," conscious at last of the fact that he didn't get on to his big job anywhere near the beginning of it. But his strong point is—nothing "rattles" him and nobody can scare him—nor hurry him.

I cannot yet definitely find out the mistake that caused me to think that you thought it desirable for me to make a brief visit home for a consultation. There's no such thing as a vacation while this earthquake continues. Fortunately I don't need one. I am, as occasion permits, driving out now and then into the country for Saturday afternoons and Sundays: that gets a change of air; and I drop the war and all its brood of woes at the third hole on a golf-course.

Many thanks for your kind letter about the marriage of my daughter. I am very content with it, since such things must be. But it's nevertheless "devilish hard on the old man." That girl has been the charm of my household here, and (if the truth were known) her mother and I need her worse than her husband does. But they are very happily paired, and that's all we have a right to ask. We all heartily appreciate your kind thought of her happiness.

No sooner had I written this than the news comes of the sinking of the *Arabic!* About this there's no use writing since all the information will promptly go by telegraph. Nobody here is in the least surprised—surely I am not. Some such thing has been expected, and more will come. Berlin is utterly desperate and it will become more desperate. The elation of success in Russia brings desperation, and so will a reverse—such a German reverse, for example, as I am now told will probably take place within a month or two at the Dardanelles. I hear that the Turks are showing unmistakable signs of exhaustion—of ammunition and of fighting qualities. The German machine has its qualities and character, which no event has yet in the slightest degree changed. It has that incurable disease—the Napoleonic ambition.

Yours sincerely,

WALTER H. PAGE.

II

What impression did these *Lusitania* telegrams and letters produce upon the statesman to whom they were addressed? This was a question that especially puzzled Page during this summer and autumn. In addition to the Ambassador's direct communications to the President, he wrote a large number of letters to Colonel House, already published in a preceding volume. These letters were written as much for President Wilson as for Colonel House. That the President's confidant would read them to his chief Page well knew; indeed they were written for that precise purpose. The more or less veiled fiction that they were addressed to a third person, gave Page great freedom in discussing the President's policies and the opinions which Great Britain and Europe held of his statesmanship. To all these letters and telegrams, however, both those sent directly and those indirectly through Colonel House, Page received no reply. He spent day after day and night after night writing letters and messages dealing with the crisis produced by Germany's unrestricted submarine warfare. Weeks and months went by, and not even an acknowledgment came from the White House. In the whole course of the war Page received only thirteen letters from Mr. Wilson. Several are extremely brief, introducing friends; others, also brief, concern merely routine matters. Only occasionally does the President make any reference to public questions, and not once does he discuss them in any detail. That President Wilson was a busy man may be taken for granted, and, to a certain degree, his failure to answer Page is explained by the great press of official business. That he was a somewhat inattentive correspondent is also no secret. Page was not the only Ambassador in a great post during the war whose confidences failed to inspire replies from the President. Yet that their contents had something to do with this Presidential indifference is probably the fact. In the early days Mr. Wilson greatly enjoyed Page's comments; as the divergence in views between the two men widened, however, his interest became less keen. Not infrequently Colonel House, visiting President Wilson after a month's or six weeks' absence from Washington, would find, among the Presidential papers, a package of Page's letters.

"Here are some letters from Page," the President would say, handing them to his adviser. "Perhaps you would like to read them."

Colonel House would take them away for perusal; occasionally he would give Mr. Wilson the gist of their contents, but not invariably. The Ambassador's views differed so from the President's own that the latter's interest was not great.

Of course, Page never knew how much or how little the President was interested. Yet the experience of

gleaned almost any good day for gossip—most of them true—but what matter? The air is full of them, clean up to the moon. But most of them are gloomy, such, for example, as the report that the British have lost 100,000 in the Dardanelles and that the late "drive" in France cost the British between 50,000 and 75,000 men. When these facts are made public in Parliament, nobody knows what sort of a convulsion will follow. Perhaps then what is known as the Northcliffe-Lloyd George conspiracy may come to a head. Certainly the Government is in deep water. There are a dozen suppressed criticisms, any one of which might (and may) cause a change of Prime Ministers and perhaps other changes almost as important—the censorship, the Dardanelles crime, the Balkan situation, conscription, etc. Except for the encouragement given by the recent advance in France, every recent military event has deepened the gloom. True, Russia is coming back, but Italy is doing nothing; will she really help in the Balkans? The Germans *may* reach Constantinople—they won't, but many persons fear they will. If the English people knew of the slaughter of their armies in France and in the Dardanelles, they would rend the Government and accept peace on almost any terms—they wouldn't of course, but the Government seem to think they would.

In these gloomy times, you will not be surprised—you have not been surprised—that the German "come-down" in the *Arabic*[1] case provoked so little comment here; for the English have destroyed so many submarines that the

[1]On September 1st, as a result of the torpedoing of the *Arabic*, Count Bernstorff handed Mr. Lansing a written pledge: "I beg to inform you that my instructions concerning our answer to your last *Lusitania* note contain the following passage: 'Liners will not be sunk by submarines without warning, and without ensuring the safety of the lives of non-combatants, provided that the liners do not try to escape or offer resistance.'"

Germans are, in that matter, at the end of their rope and they are using us to save their face. It's a moral certainty that the submarine which sunk the *Arabic* was itself sunk on that very day and there were no survivors. "Commander Schneider" is as dead as Rip Van Winkle's dog. But the English are interested in the *Lusitania* case. They say, "She was sunk nearly six months ago, and no satisfactory answer has yet been given about her—how long can the Germans keep the President waiting?" "Remember the *Lusitania*" was one of the most successful recruiting circulars during the early summer, and it has more than once been the battle-cry of attacking British forces in France. We shall not get credit in English opinion for a decisive diplomatic victory over Germany until the *Lusitania* case is satisfactorily closed. . . .

I see and feel in a hundred ways and am reminded by a hundred incidents of a considerable drifting apart of our people and the English—not unnatural at all, but in a degree delicate: I do not think dangerous. But it must be handled with care. Here they are on the border of a panic about the war—perhaps also on the verge of a political upheaval. The task is too great for their organization and they are not clever at organization as a rule, nor quick. All day every day we work with their difficulties and their sorrows—concrete cases of dead and wounded and prisoners; and we live in the atmosphere (for that matter, in the very area) of war. . . . In official life you hear a few ghastly and disquieting secrets, and every man there is worked to death. Sir Edward Grey hasn't slept more than a few hours for nearly a week. . . . On the outskirts of official life you hear of this impending change and that—that Sir Edward has failed and must go, that Lord Kitchener is a stuffed dummy, that Lloyd George, though a wind-bag, is the best man they have, and so on, *ad nauseam* and *ad infinitum*.

Out of this atmosphere I go to the Foreign Office to insist on the immediate release of a cargo of toys waiting in Rotterdam. I am patiently listened to; but the next day I learn (thro' the back door) that one of the Under-Secretaries, when he was told what I asked, remarked, "Last Christmas the Americans were giving us all, including the Germans, a ship-load of toys. Now they are quarrelling because they can't get a ship-load from Germany—odd Yankees, aren't they?" This afternoon's paper lectures us on our imbecility in trying to save the Armenians—or (as it puts it) in trying "by the most valiant use of words."—They are on the borderland of a panic. John Morley, who hadn't before been heard of since the war began, appeared in the House of Lords yesterday and asked questions that might cause half the Cabinet to fall, if they were to be pressed home with sufficient vigour. . . .

To descend to a much smaller aspect of the same subject, there is an indescribable strain on the nerves of all men here: nobody is built for this kind of thing. A few days ago a little group, chiefly of medical men but partly also of military men and civilians, gave a good-bye luncheon to the American physician who has for a year been at the head of the Red Cross American hospital in this kingdom. Apropos of nothing in particular, almost every man at the table began to weep. Osler wiped his eyes time and again, and the General who sat next me said in a weeping whisper: "I've got to get back to the War Office to my work—can't stand this sort of thing." . . .

Your faithful friend,
WALTER H. PAGE.

To the President

London, December 31, 1915.

DEAR MR. PRESIDENT:

My Christmas guess, of no particular value, but as good as anybody else's, is that the war will end next summer or autumn—sooner only if some decisive military event give the Germans a good excuse to make terms. We live in a censored world here—in a sort of fog; but there are too many signs of impending German disaster to doubt its coming: this in spite of the extraordinary series of bad failures by the Allies—the Dardanelles failure, the Balkan failure, two military failures in France when the German line was actually broken. These failures have singularly little effect on the English, whose slow stupidity one curses with the more vehemence and whose cool endurance one admires with the more confidence the more one sees of them. The upshot of it is they are invincible, but they bungle their work so that a victory is far, far more costly than it ought to be. They think that the all-around changes they have just made in their military commands are great improvements. I can form no opinion about that; but anybody can see that some sort of change was desirable.

There is great dissatisfaction, too, with the Government; but there's no way to change it except by the voluntary resignation of the Ministers. The Prime Minister will not resign (his wife said the other day that "nobody but God could put Herbert out"); and Sir Edward Grey's resignation will not be accepted by him. It is against these two that the fiercest criticism continues to beat—against Asquith because the war doesn't go forward fast enough and because he doesn't seem to deal frankly with the people, and against Grey for the diplomatic failure to secure the Balkan States to the Allies. But during those months the English were thinking chiefly of keeping the Germans out of Calais and of holding the German line in France till the Russians should threaten—Berlin! The story goes about now that the Turks offered to permit the British to go through the Dardanelles for the payment of a sum that is small in comparison with what the Dardanelles failure cost. The answer they got was that the English do not do things in that way. The Navy and Army regard Sir Edward Grey, who is supposed to be responsible for this answer, as a visionary statesman—"too much of a gentleman," as old Lord Fisher said of Mr. Balfour.

Of course, we who are onlookers here have long ago passed the place where we can be surprised by any event; but unless new and disastrous things happen in the Balkans or beyond, I have good hope that Sir Edward will not be driven out of office till the war end. He will then go because his eyes demand rest. Else he may go blind. I lay stress on this because his continuing in office is of prime importance to us. He sees more nearly eye-to-eye with us than (I think) any other member of the Cabinet. He has to yield to his associates, who reflect and represent British opinion about the uses of sea power; and especially does he have to yield to the military and naval group and to the lawyer group. But he has softened many a blow. The diplomatic corps here share my estimate of him. Within the last few days Allied and neutral diplomats alike have expressed to me the greatest alarm lest he should resign in disgust at the criticism of him which comes from half the points of the compass. I don't think the diplomats now in service command great weight or brains. I fear that one has a tendency to lessen his list of great men as he sees them at close range. But, as nearly as I can judge, the group in London make a higher average by a good deal than the group at any other capital. Imperiali, the Italian Ambassador, dined with me three nights ago, and I could get him to talk about nothing else than Sir Edward. Merry del Val, the Spaniard, gave me a call lasting a whole working morning, to express his alarm. The Minister from X . . . danced all around the room muttering his fear, "God knows we have a hard enough time now. But with Curzon, who can tell what we should suffer?" And it's Curzon they talk about for the Foreign Office if a change should be made.

Those of us who have so far fought thro' this war have long ago got past the least trace of awe of noble lords, or vice-gerents, or royalty; but you don't want—for steady intercourse—to deal with a fellow who has an air of ordering all mundane things; you're afraid you'll be tempted some day to say what you think of him, which wouldn't be diplomatic. In India Curzon quarrelled with Kitchener—which I secretly hold to his credit. For nobody seems able to work with Kitchener. For twenty years he ordered savages and dependent nations about. The people believe him great and the Government used him most effectively. His name raised a great army, Lord Derby actually doing the work. Thus, you see, we live not in an ordered world, but in a world of ragged hopes and fears. I fancy that History, in one of her vagaries, will set down these plausibilities for facts—that Asquith was England's greatest Prime Minister and that Grey failed in the great war as Secretary for Foreign Affairs—both wide of the truth.

I've heard nothing lately about the British reply to our long Note. I know they are looking up facts for a reply, and I'll ask when I see Sir Edward next—in a day or two.

ally. He loses twice as many men on every move as he need lose. Man for man, he is worth five Germans—alone. In an army every German is worth five Englishmen. This sort of fighting, therefore, *can* be carried on for years and years. Fowler sometimes thinks it may. Both sides lack initiative. Both sides have Old World faults. The Australians, New Zealanders, and Canadians (being Englishmen set free) are by far the best soldiers in this war. This American youth is like them. When he was appointed on the Colonel's staff, he begged and begged to command a gun till he got it. He's there to do the effective work—not for safety. There's little chance, I fear, that he will come out whole—or come out at all. When he goes, he'll be gone forever.[1] Kipling said, when his boy went off: "I'll never see him again," and now he's dead.

This estimate of the English by Fowler is startlingly accurate. They lack knack. Else, they'd end the job quickly. They lack knack at all *new* tasks. That's the trouble with their government in war time. They manage their finances and their navy incomparably—two tasks they've done for centuries—continuously done. I came near writing that they muddle everything else: I think they do.

A very well-informed Dane from Copenhagen—an Under Secretary in one department of his government—told me last night after dinner and cigars, that he often fears that the English will drive the Danes into the war on the German side by their stupidity about preventing Danish trade—in spite of the fact that every three Danes out of four are pro-British. I am told his judgment may be twisted by the trade troubles that he has to handle.

[1] This prophecy was happily not fulfilled; Mr. Fowler came out of the war in good condition.

But he said that he knew the Germans were building twenty-four gigantic submarines. When they are ready they will come out for ships to and from the United States much farther out at sea than the scene of the *Lusitania* and *Arabic* attacks and consequently farther from danger of British attack.[1]

Well, my poor letter is dwindling down to mere gossip, and it's the dullest week of the year in London. Let me add my most hearty good wishes to you and Mrs. Wilson for the New Year and for all New Years. We keep in our trenches here with good spirits and unwearying efforts; and contrary to the predictions of wiser men, I still hope that the war will end in 1916. Yet I confess I fear the wiser men who say 1917 or 1918 may guess better than I.

Sincerely yours,
WALTER H. PAGE.

---

[1]Just as I am about to seal this, private information comes from Liverpool that German submarines have sunk several British ships in the Irish Sea during the past week. (W. H. P.'s note.)

CHAPTER X

I

IN THE early part of January, 1916, Colonel House arrived in London. Nothing was said publicly about the purpose of the visit, but that purpose was hardly concealed. President Wilson was renewing his efforts to end the war. The whole proceeding caused Page the greatest misgiving. By this time the Ambassador had lost faith in the wisdom of President Wilson's leadership. He had tried to see the President's point of view, to sympathize with his attempts to solve the *Lusitania* crisis without involving the country in war, and to believe that back of what Page regarded as Mr. Wilson's inadequacy and indecision there lay a wise and far-reaching policy. Now, however, the facts proved too strong for Page. As he passed in review the events of eighteen months, the aspect that chiefly appalled him was Mr. Wilson's apparent disposition to deal gently with the Germans. Page did not necessarily regard the President as pro-German, yet the anti-British note which, the Ambassador believed, he could always feel in American foreign policy, caused him the deepest anxiety. In practically every question since 1914 the inevitable effect of the American attitude was to make things easier for Germany and more difficult for Great Britain. This was the case with the Declaration of London, with the *Dacia*, and the correspondence about the blockade, and with the failure to adopt a vigorous course in the *Lusitania* crisis and the submarine campaign.

Meanwhile other happenings had added to Page's dissatisfaction with the Administration. The long drawn-out argument over the *Lusitania* seemed to be approaching its end; Bernstorff and Mr. Lansing had apparently hit upon some plan for settling that question; just what the plan was no one knew, but that it did not comprise a disavowal by Germany and an admission of guilt was no secret. Such a settlement, Page believed, would only add to the humiliation of the United States; moreover, he did not think that even in the reparation Germany was then discussing, as a matter of grace rather than as a matter of justice, her motives were at all sincere; one object, perhaps the compelling one, was to end an inconvenient quarrel with the United States, in the expectation that Mr. Wilson, having extracted these concessions from Germany, would concentrate all his energies on his disputes with Great Britain. The great German goal, as ever, was to use the United States to end the blockade. The uninterrupted transmission of essential war supplies from American to neutral ports, whence they could quickly be sent to Germany, was becoming more and more essential to German success. The hope of attaining this purpose, or, failing that, to cause a breach between Great Britain and the United States, was, as Page regarded the pending *Lusitania* negotiations, the real purpose of the unsatisfactory concessions which Germany was evidently prepared to make.

Another incident—an incident which only a few persons then knew anything about and which is made public for the first time in this Presidential correspondence—was always present in Page's mind, and did more perhaps than even the *Lusitania* controversy to break down his confi-

dence in the Wilson administration. In the latter part of
September, 1915, Mr. Alexander C. Kirk, Secretary at
the American Embassy in Berlin, appeared in London and
immediately reported to Mr. Irwin Laughlin. Mr. Kirk's
story was of such an unprecedented character that Mr.
Laughlin at once conducted him to the Ambassador. He
was the bearer of a parcel of documents which Mr. James
W. Gerard, American Ambassador at Berlin, regarded as
so important and so dangerous that he would not take the
risk of making any telegraphic or written communication
concerning them. Hence he had dispatched them to Page
by one of his own secretaries. Page examined the documents, and immediately sent the following telegram to
Washington:

To the Secretary of State

London, September 25, 1915.

SECRETARY OF STATE,
    Washington.
        2855, September 25, 2 P. M.
    Confidential for the Secretary.
    Referring to package of papers forwarded in depart-
ment pouch to Berlin which you instructed Gerard to
return to you personally, I transmit the following telegram, written by Kirk, Third Secretary of Berlin Embassy, who has come here under Gerard's oral instructions
to send it, as it could not safely be dispatched from Berlin.
Kirk remains here pending your instructions. Papers are
in my safe.
    "Package in question which has been placed with other
official notes pending receipt of instructions from the
Department, was inadvertently opened by Mr. Gerard
himself and as importance of contents was instantly
perceived, all papers were examined. Package found to

contain statements in duplicate of accounts of German Embassy in Washington together with supporting vouchers in the original or certified copy. Vouchers show that $5,000 was paid to Archibald for propaganda, $4,500 to Marcus Braun, editor of *Fair Play*, $3,000 to Miss Ray Beveridge for a lecture tour, and $1,000 to Edwin Emerson for travelling expenses. In addition statements from the Western Union Telegraph-Cable Company contain names of persons in the United States and elsewhere to whom messages were sent by the German Embassy, as well as purpose of message, whether propaganda or official business. These statements show also the bill for cables to Bogotá from April first to the tenth amounted to over four thousand dollars and to Guatemala three thousand and to Shanghai two thousand. Large sums spent in cables to Mexico City, Manila, Honolulu, Haiti, and Buenos Aires in that paper appear to furnish authentic list of all kinds of German agents in the United States and elsewhere and also indicate extent and direction of German propaganda.

"In this connection, Mr. Gerard considers that Department would be justified in examining papers in question, especially in view of the fact that since beginning of war, American Embassy in Berlin has found it necessary to direct seventeen notes to the German Foreign Office protesting against opening of mail addressed to the Ambassador. These protests have, for most part, been ignored, while in the single case where a letter to another Chief of Mission in Berlin was opened, an official apology was made before protest was lodged.

"Mr. Gerard, in accordance with his custom in opening correspondence, did not tear envelopes or break seals of this parcel but detached bottom flap of envelope without it.

"In view of nature of documents it did not seem advisable to photograph them in Berlin or entrust them to regular courier."

AMERICAN AMBASSADOR,
London.

The documents which Mr. Kirk had brought from Mr. Gerard in Berlin to Page were the records of Count Bernstorff, German Ambassador to the United States, containing the financial details of his propaganda activities in the United States and other countries. They showed his disbursement of $5,000 to J. F. J. Archibald, the American journalist in German and Austrian pay, whose papers, recently intercepted and published by the British, had caused the dismissal of Doctor Dumba as Austrian Ambassador to the United States. They disclosed Bernstorff's payments to many other persons engaged, in the United States and elsewhere, in spreading German propaganda; indeed, they gave a complete picture of Bernstorff using his ambassadorial post at Washington as a headquarters for conducting a lively campaign, throughout the world, in favour of German purposes and in hostility to the United States. Practically all the agents mentioned by Count Bernstorff had been attacking American war-time policy, in some instances personally assailing President Wilson; here was the proof, in the form of official German documents, that the German Ambassador had been financing these attacks; here, indeed, were Count Bernstorff's records of his disbursements for that purpose. More extraordinary still, it appeared that Mr. Gerard had uncovered these incriminating papers in the American diplomatic pouch, sent from the State Department to Berlin. In what manner had all this evidence found its way into so inappropriate a habitat? One would have concluded that fate had played a sorry trick on Bernstorff in placing the facts that were more than sufficient to destroy his diplomatic career in the one place where they could do him the most harm, and that correspondingly it had done the American Government a great kindness in thus delivering its enemy into its hands.

Subsequent events disclosed, however, that fortune had had nothing to do with this transaction. The man who had entrusted these confidential documents to the American diplomatic pouch was none other than Count Bernstorff himself. One day in early September, probably about the time that popular excitement over the Dumba disclosure was most keen, Ambassador Bernstorff called at the State Department. He had a package, the German Ambassador said, which he wished to forward to Germany in the Department's official mail bag. Would the Department consent to send it? Count Bernstorff treated the matter as unimportant, and gave the impression that the papers in question concerned trifling and routine administrative details. Permission having been obtained, he delivered a sealed envelope, which was put in the Department's pouch and in due course reached Mr. Gerard. Mr. Gerard opened it, in the somewhat ingenious manner Mr. Kirk describes in his message. Even though Mr. Gerard had observed that it was addressed to the German Foreign Minister, he would have had every right to investigate; for it came in the American pouch, and an Ambassador is entitled to know what documents he has been asked to transmit. The resultant "find," however, astonished and shocked Mr. Gerard. Obviously he could not deliver the papers to their appointed destination; the information in them was something that his government was entitled to receive; the only course was to return them to Washington. But he could not send such dangerous papers from Berlin; the risk of discovery was too great. This is the reason that he very judiciously dispatched them, by the hand of a trusted courier, to Page for transmission to Mr. Lansing.

Page at once sent the papers to the State Department. They were immediately forwarded again to Mr. Gerard, with instructions to hand them to the German Foreign Secretary.

Page refers to this proceeding several times in his letters. It really preyed upon his mind. That the State Department had obtained first-hand evidence disclosing Bernstorff's subversive activities in the United States, and still failed to demand the Ambassador's recall, was only one aspect that shocked him. Above all was his humiliating discovery of the contempt and cynicism with which the German Ambassador treated the Administration. Bernstorff evidently regarded the State Department with so little seriousness that he used it for transmitting his most secret papers,—and papers that betrayed his plottings against the country whose hospitality he enjoyed. In Page's view the act of Mr. Lansing—and presumably of the President—in persisting in sending these documents to the German Government, after Page, in accordance with Mr. Gerard's request, had sent them to Washington, simply showed that they were prepared to resort to all means, even to the suppression of evidence, in their determination to avoid a rupture with Germany. Coming after a long course of similar happenings, it destroyed any remaining confidence Page may have had in Mr. Wilson's desire to protect American interest and honour, and henceforth it influenced all his thinking and writing about the President. In part it accounts for the tone of the memorandum which he wrote about Colonel House's visit to London in January, 1916:

Events crowd one another.

Lunch to-day: Sir Edward Grey, Lord Robert Cecil, House, Laughlin, and I. House said: "The United States would like Great Britain to do whatever would help the United States to aid the Allies," and he said that this is the way the President feels. Much talk along the same line. House made it plain, however, that if the President openly came out for the Allies, he could not command the public sentiment of the country. This (as matters stand to-day with Congress in session) is no doubt literally true. But it raises a deeper question. That is to say, public sentiment is now neutral and to a great degree not interested in the war. But is not this the result of the President's own work in preaching the duty of personal neutrality? Suppose the President had contented himself with declaring the neutrality of the Government, with seeing to it that the Government was really neutral, but had refrained, in his several speeches and in his Messages, from exhorting the people to a strict personal neutrality—suppose he had refrained from labouring our detachment and our unconcern—wouldn't there have been a better general understanding of the war and a stronger and more general natural feeling for the Allies than there now is? This is a point of much importance. Hasn't the President done all he could to *make* the people detached? Then, after that event, isn't House using their detachment as an explanation of his detached conduct? There has somewhere in this business been a lack of such leadership as the President showed about the domestic issues of the early part of his Administration.

The President to-day sends House a telegram to the effect that the German submarine controversy being laid, all the pressure of criticism will be made on Great Britain —a certain fierce, blue-bellied Presbyterian tone in it.

And the *Lusitania* and all the other submarine troubles do seem composed—to the point of American acceptance at least. The Germans stoop to conquer. Bernstorff is hailed as a sort of hero, who has brought his own government to meet the American demands. The text of the German answer and pledge has not yet been made public— it has gone to Berlin for ratification. But there's no doubt about a "settlement" having been reached. There is an insincerity about it because it has been reached only in order to begin an attack on Great Britain. In other words, our government is used by Bernstorff as a tool against Great Britain. In the last analysis, this is beyond all question. There's bound at some time to be a rebound from this position: it isn't sincere on the part of the Germans and it isn't quite satisfying to American pride and to the American conscience.

A lack of leadership, for instance, crops out in this "profound secret" which House tells me. Gerard some time ago had a long conversation with the Kaiser. He wrote to the President that he was not at liberty to repeat the Kaiser's remarks! But he enclosed in his letter a cryptic sentence on a separate sheet which said that "after this war, I will give attention to the United States"[1] —how instead of commanding Gerard to report what the Emperor said, the President asks House to go to Berlin and find out!—and find out whether he meant this as a threat. Now if there hadn't been a mortal dread of war and therefore a mortal dread of Germany, such a procedure would not have been adopted.

The facts strongly implied and morally proved, if not technically proved, by the "accounts"—i. e., financial papers—which Lansing permitted Bernstorff to send to

---

[1]Ambassador Gerard tells of this famous interview in his book, "My Four Years in Germany," Chapter XII, p. 252.

Berlin in our pouch (and which Gerard sent all the way back to Washington and which Lansing again sent to Berlin in our pouch)—these facts were a strong enough conviction of Bernstorff to warrant his dismissal. But they have been pigeon-holed. Now, Von Papen, the dismissed German military attaché, while on his way home was searched at Falmouth, and his checks and check books were taken from him.

From London Colonel House went to Paris and Berlin. He returned to London in February with a definite scheme for obtaining peace. What this plan was and the opinion of it entertained by the Ambassador appear in the following memorandum.

Memorandum, dated February 9, 1916

House arrived from Berlin—Paris—Havre (the King of the Belgians) full of the idea of American intervention. First his plan was that he and I and a group of the British Cabinet (Grey, Asquith, Lloyd George, Reading, etc.) should at once work out a minimum programme of peace— the least that the Allies would accept, which, he assumed, would be unacceptable to the Germans; and that the President would take this programme and present it to both sides; the side that declined would be responsible for continuing the war. Then, to end the war, the President would help the other side—that is, the Allies. House had talked more or less with some members of the French Government, who, he said, were enthusiastic about it. I wonder if they understood what he said, or whether he understood what they said? Then, too, the King of the Belgians approved it. Of course, the fatal moral weakness of the foregoing scheme is that we should plunge into the war, not on the merits of the cause, but by a carefully sprung trick. When I said that the way to get into the war was for a proper cause—to decline to be hoodwinked about the *Lusitania* or (or and) to send Bernstorff home because he gave money to Von Papen which went to bomb-throwers, etc., etc.—of which the Department of State has documentary evidence—*this* is the way to get into the war—then House objected that we must do it the President's own way. Of course such an indirect scheme is doomed to failure—is wrong, in fact.

Of course, too, as I told House, nobody here would dare talk about peace, and that, if they *did* dare, nobody would dare accept the President's "intervention." They no longer have confidence in the President.

The next day (Thursday, February 10th) House told me that the better plan would be simply to have the President invite both sides to hold a conference and let them work it out themselves—as if they would now confer!

House told me that we'd have a meeting on Monday—Asquith, Grey, Reading, Lloyd George, he, and I. No, we won't. No member of the Government can afford to discuss any such subject; not one of them has any confidence in the strength of the President for action.

Therefore on Friday, 11 February, I told House that I couldn't go with him to any such conference, and I wouldn't.

He didn't seem surprised; for (I think) he had discovered that such a conference was either impossible or dangerous. He confessed that he was "uneasy on every account."

This memorandum gives only a faint conception of Page's mood at that time. In his discussion with English-

men, and even with the members of his own staff, he
maintained a strict diplomatic reserve; it was characteristic of his frank nature, however, that, in setting forth his
views with the President's personal representative, he
should not mince matters to the slightest degree. The
fact is that recent events had completely exhausted his
patience. The contempt shown by Bernstorff for the
United States, and the failure of the President to resent
this contempt, was a sore wound to Page's proud American
soul. What he looked upon as the indirection of this
latest peace proposal also stirred him deeply. Blessed by
Heaven with great facility of speech—sometimes almost
to a disconcerting extent—he now unburdened himself
in a quarter where his outspokenness at least could not
subject him to the charge of deceit—to President Wilson's
closest personal confidant. Page spent one whole evening with Colonel House discussing the President's war
policy, taking it up point by point from the day the Germans invaded Belgium. Striding up and down his room,
speaking with the rapidity that marked his utterance in
his intense and excited moments, Page on this memorable
evening characterized each step in the Wilsonian war
programme. From the beginning, the whole thing seemed
to him a gigantic calamity. The criticisms Page had been
writing Colonel House and the President he now repeated in the most expressive language. He could find
only one episode in American history which compared
with Wilson's behaviour in the war. Page had been a
student of Jefferson from his boyhood; his favourite ideas
on social organization he had obtained from his favourite
philosopher of democracy; in certain aspects Jefferson
had been the inspiration of his life. But his admiration
for the great Virginian was not one-sided; it was dis-
criminating to a degree. There was one chapter in

honour, our own interests, our own position in the world to maintain. If we were going to war, Page believed, we should go to war in the first place to maintain that dignity and honour; the self-respect of the nation demanded straightforward action, not a roundabout approach to the great subject.

Page felt so deeply that, as he records, he refused to attend the dinner at which the proposal was to be discussed. The meeting nevertheless was held at the house of Lord Reading, at that time Chancellor of the Exchequer. Page was entirely right about the prevailing attitude of the British popular mind toward peace. Emotion ran so high in London that it was necessary to observe the utmost secrecy. "If it were known that we were meeting for the purpose of discussing peace," remarked Sir Edward Grey to Colonel House, "every window in my house would be smashed." It is only recently indeed that the world has learned that, in February, 1916, the foremost leaders of the British Empire, Mr. Asquith, Sir Edward Grey, Mr. Arthur J. Balfour, Mr. Lloyd George, and Lord Reading quietly met one evening with Colonel House to consider a plan that had two alternatives: either a peace fairly satisfactory to the Allies or the entrance into the war of the United States on their side. It was proposed to offer Germany a choice that was essentially an ultimatum: accept this settlement of the war, or accept America as an enemy in arms! This plan is the one embodied in a document that promises to become historic as the "House Memorandum." Lord Grey has made it public for the first time in his book, "Twenty-five Years." The paper, as Lord Grey publishes it, was the joint production of himself and Colonel House. It is significantly dated on Washington's birthday, 1916.

Memorandum

(Confidential)

Colonel House told me that President Wilson was ready, on hearing from France and England, to propose that a conference should be summoned to put an end to the war. Should the Allies accept this proposal, and should Germany refuse it, the United States would probably enter the war against Germany.

Colonel House expressed the opinion that, if such a conference met, it would secure peace on terms not unfavourable to the Allies; and if it failed to secure peace, the United States would leave the Conference as a belligerent on the side of the Allies, if Germany was unreasonable. Colonel House expressed an opinion decidedly favourable to the restoration of Belgium, the transfer of Alsace and Lorraine to France, and the acquisition by Russia of an outlet to the sea, though he thought that the lost territory incurred by Germany in one place would have to be compensated to her by concessions to her in other places outside Europe. If the Allies delayed accepting the offer of President Wilson, and if, later on, the course of the war was so unfavourable to them that the intervention of the United States would not be effective, the United States would probably disinterest themselves in Europe and look to their protection in their own way.

I said that I felt the statement, coming from the President of the United States, to be a matter of such importance that I must inform the Prime Minister and my colleagues; but that I could say nothing until it had received their consideration. The British Government could, under no circumstances, accept or make any proposal except in consultation and agreement with the

Allies. I thought that the Cabinet would probably feel that the present situation would not justify them in approaching their allies on this subject at the present moment; but, as Colonel House had an intimate conversation with M. Briand and M. Jules Cambon in Paris, I should think it right to tell M. Briand privately, through the French Ambassador in London, what Colonel House had said to us; and I should, of course, whenever there was an opportunity, be ready to talk the matter over with M. Briand, if he desired it.[1]

E. G.

The reference to M. Briand concerns an important meeting between that French statesman, then Prime Minister and Minister of Foreign Affairs, and Colonel House, in the course of the American's recent visit to Paris. At that time Colonel House informed the French Premier that the United States had no intention of standing aside if it became apparent that abstention from war would result in a German victory. This conversation was really a commitment by the United States to France of an unprecedented kind. The United States wished to be informed if, and when, our military assistance was needed to prevent the triumph of Germany. Any time the French Government would notify Washington that our aid was indispensable, then this aid would be forthcoming. The only condition President Wilson demanded was that he receive this notification in time to make American assistance decisive. If word came at too late a date to give this country any chance of aiding effectively, then we could not regard it. In other words, the United States wished to enter a going concern, not a bankrupt one. The proposal amounted to a demand that France, in case

---

[1]"Twenty-five Years," by Viscount Grey of Fallodon; Vol. II, pages 127-128.

she was able to see her approaching destruction far enough ahead, should, so to speak, sound the tocsin, in which case this country would hasten to her assistance. The French Republic never sent Washington such a message.

Of the several statesmen present at this meeting at Lord Reading's house, Grey was the only one who positively endorsed the proposal embodied in the "House Memorandum." On the other hand, not one spoke against it, and the sentiment, on the whole, was rather favourable. All expressed an opinion except Lord Reading, who merely sat and listened. Lloyd George talked much and laid the utmost emphasis upon the influence of Wilson. The world situation, he declared, lay in the President's hands; he could make peace at any time and practically dictate the terms of settlement. Asquith's attitude was non-committal although he displayed no hostility to the plan.

In the interest of strict historic accuracy, however, it must be pointed out that the proposal so secretly discussed that evening was not identically the one which is printed in the memoirs of Lord Grey. This text contains an important word that did not appear in the original version. The document, as drawn by Colonel House and the Foreign Secretary, was taken to Washington by Colonel House and laid before the President. The President, Lord Grey relates, approved it and sent it back to London with only one change. Lord Grey does not disclose just what the change made by President Wilson was, but it may be revealed in this place. As the paper came to the President the last sentence of the first paragraph ran thus: "Should the Allies accept this proposal, and should Germany refuse it, the United States would enter the war against Germany." This phrasing, of course, made the document an absolute commitment by the United States. Between the words "would" and "enter" the President now inserted the word "probably"; so that the important phrase read, "The United States would *probably* enter the war."

It is not likely that Page ever saw this memorandum, either before or after it had been subjected to Presidential revision; as his own memorandum shows, however, he was acquainted with its substance and strongly disapproved. Opinions may differ as to his judgment, but on one point at least he was right—the plan proved utterly futile. In Page's mind, this scheme simply amounted to trifling with a subject of the most momentous consequence. The unfortunate fact is that Page had no longer any confidence in President Wilson. Had he seen the memorandum, after the President had inserted a word that changed the whole document from a definite pledge to a conditional one—one that still, after the preliminary steps had been taken, left the President free to retreat before the irrevocable step—Page would unquestionably have regarded that change as merely confirming his lack of faith. He would have looked upon it as another instance of that indecision, that inability to do anything positive which, in his opinion, had marked the President's course from the first. There were other reasons why the Ambassador would have looked on this outline of peace as an inadequate programme. The European situation, the Ambassador well understood, made impracticable any attempt to end the war on this basis. The "House Memorandum" did not sufficiently regard the complexities of European politics. Great Britain was not the only Allied power; in particular there was France. Lord Grey relates that the substance of this document was communicated to France through the French Ambassador in London, but that France ignored it.   That the proposal would be unwelcome to Frenchmen may be assumed. This memorandum did not contemplate the complete defeat of Germany; its acceptance would have been a humiliation for the Fatherland, it is true, for the cession of Alsace-Lorraine to France and of Constantinople to Russia would have seemed something almost inconceivable in face of the existing military strength of Germany. Still, peace on these terms would not have represented the final triumph that France regarded as essential to her safety as a nation.   The very existence of their country, Frenchmen believed, depended on the destruction of Germany as a military power.   France had succeeded in consolidating Great Britain, Italy, and Russia as Allies in this war.   French statesmen believed that this was something they would never be able to do again. They were therefore convinced that if they could not utterly defeat Germany this time, they could never accomplish it; on the other hand, unless they did defeat Germany, they believed that France as an independent nation had come to its end.   Any halfway measures with Germany, even though they represented great German concessions, would merely postpone for a short time the collapse of their country.   The American proposal for ending the war did not aim at any such unquestioned destruction of German military power.   It left intact the German Army, the German Navy, the German industrial and military machine.   Peace on these terms would mean that Germany would be able to recuperate her forces and economic strength, and in the course of ten or fifteen years, or perhaps earlier, start the war again.   In the beginning Page had insisted, as had most observers, that any peace which left the way open to a resumption of the conflict in any appreciable time, would be worse than the continuation of the existing war. President Wilson's new proposal did not guarantee France from a renewal of the attack. And when this second attack came would Great Britain, Italy, and Russia take the field as her allies? French statesmen had no confidence that such an alliance could be reformed. They therefore pictured themselves, a decade or so hence, again assailed by the Central Empires—France this time standing alone, without great allies; they knew they would be defeated and that France would go down in ruin. This is the reason why France could not accept any terms of peace which did not mean the end of German military power. She would rather take the chance of being defeated in this war than accept such a peace, because she knew that in ten years or fifteen years it was probable that she would be destroyed. Frenchmen regarded French salvation as dependent upon a continuation of this struggle, even under the discouraging conditions that prevailed in February, 1916, because they might still get the United States in and thereby win the victory which would eliminate Germany as a danger. This was the reason that the House Memorandum was ignored by France.

The situation of Great Britain, however, was quite different. Britain's future did not depend upon the annihilation of the German Army; she still had her great fleet and her dominions and therefore was secure from any fear of destruction. Moreover, a large part of the thinking British public did not look with any particular satisfaction upon a victorious Russia; in their view a peace that would leave Russia in a weak position would be better for Great Britain than one which would leave the Tsar as a military menace to the British Empire. For these reasons the terms of peace proposed by Colonel House, which amounted to a victory over Germany—

though not an overwhelming one—would have been fairly satisfactory. Yet the behaviour of the British Foreign Office toward France was entirely honourable. For the very reason that a knockout was necessary for French security but not for British, the British statesmen could not be urgent in asking France to accept this document as a basis for bringing the war to an end. This is the explanation for Grey's action in merely transmitting the suggestion to France, making no recommendation when he did so, and, when France ignored it, the plan naturally expired.

II

Embassy of the United States of America,
12 May, 1916, London.

DEAR MR. PRESIDENT:

The message that you were kind enough to telegraph about Shakespeare[1] was enthusiastically received at the Mansion House meeting, whereat men representing most countries (other than the German, of course) paid their countries' tribute to the poet; and I have had many persons speak to me since about it. It added just the right American touch to a notable meeting.

A word about Colonel Squier, for four years our military attaché here, whom the War Department has just called home for service in the Department. Squier, a West Point man, is also a Ph. D. of Johns Hopkins—in Physics. He was under Rowland. He made a great place for him-

---

[1]On March 6, 1916, Page wrote the President telling him of the plans for the celebration, on April 23rd, of the tercentenary of Shakespeare's birth, and asking for a message to be read at a meeting at the Mansion House. President Wilson sent the following telegram:

"I join with all lovers of great literature in unqualified admiration of the great genius which spoke the human spirit in fuller measure and more authoritative tones than any other man of any race or age."

self here. I think he belongs to more learned scientific societies in England than any other American. He is one of our most distinguished physicists, and his inventions in telegraphy—with especial reference to cables and cable service—have brought him the friendship of all the great scientific men in the kingdom. The British Government is now using an invention of his which doubles the service of every cable it has. Characteristically Squier simply made them a present of it till the war ends. He has, therefore, added real distinction to this Embassy—in a most unusual way. Besides, he seems to be as good a military man as he is a scientific investigator. The army men here hold him in the greatest esteem. He has Kitchener's frank confidence. He was the guest for weeks of the British Headquarters in France. The reports that he has prepared for our War Department and the War College, will, I am told, be the textbooks on military subjects hereafter. A British General asked me the other day, apropos of Squier's going home, why such a man in our army was not promoted. "Squier a mere Lieutenant Colonel! If we had him, we'd make him a Brigadier General, a Lieutenant General, a General, or a Field Marshall." I take the liberty to suggest that you send for him. He can tell you more about the military situation than any other man I know. By the way, his permanent successor here ought not to be a man of lower rank than a Colonel—of higher rank if possible. It is hard for you and me, who have smiled at ranks and gold lace all our lives, to appreciate the immeasurable distance here between a Captain (say) and a Brigadier General. It is quite as great a difference as between a stenographer in the War Department and the Secretary of War.

The English ought to be drawn and quartered for their sluggish stupidity in forever abusing one another and for forever grumbling. They seem to have (with their Allies, all of whom they maintain by money and supplies) the military situation well in hand. The Germans have had a hard blow and a serious setback at Verdun. In spite of that, the prevalent English mood is a mood of depression. They fear that they can never win a real victory but only a draw—and this just when they have voted for conscription and can thus continue to put men into the field— a larger reserve than Germany has. Waves of feeling sweep over them as billows break on a rocky shore. But the rock remains after the billows are all gone—luckily for them. My own belief is that the only invincible thing in Europe are these same English. If all Europe were against them instead of the Germans, still they'd win in the long run. Yet they wrangle and become "grouchy" and decline even to permit their friends to know what they are doing. I could with truth tell the whole race what I've often told groups of them—that they are good for nothing except to become ancestors of Americans and Colonials. In America and their large colonies, the English become free and hopeful. The despair, the depression, the melancholy, the slow ichor in the blood— of all Europeans, with the possible exception of the French—is what damns them all. It turns their eyes inward and backward. And yet these are the only invincible people in this world—this race. Perhaps I've told you that I talk with many women who have come to ask me to have inquiries made about their sons and husbands who are "missing." "Missing" generally means dead, and that is what they all fear. But they hope that it may mean imprisonment. They tell their stories with the same fortitude, the same self-restraint, the same sorrowful pride—noblewomen and working women alike. The Spartan women were weaklings beside the English. I daily grow stronger in my Americanism—real Americanism, not the hyphenated counterfeit. For the British race is the best race yet mixed and developed on this globe, and this race comes to its best under freer and more mobile conditions than this rainy isle of dukes and earls permits. People here now discuss everything with reference to "after the war." "What are we going to do after the war? What do we do best?" I have an easy answer. "Send your children to the United States. Your daughters will become handsomer and your sons more adaptable—they'll be English set free: that's what an American is. The best thing you've ever done is to breed men for freer lands." And they believe it—some of 'em do at least. These English are the most interesting study in the world. Just when you'd like to hang them for their stupidity, you become aware of such noble stuff in them that you thank God that they were your ancestors. And Europe would be a bloody slave pen to-day but for them. It's a shambles as it is.

They are not going to get tired. Peace? Yes, on their terms. And, while they are fighting for their lives, they are the only nation that is not fighting also for booty. And among many things that this war is teaching them is the stupidity of their arrogance when they twice provoked us to war. They pathetically yearn for our utmost good-will—even while they (some of them at least) curse us. My admiration for their racial qualities deepens while my impatience with their ways is heightened. I could write a book in worship of them and another book damning them—both true, both concrete, both definitely proving my thesis.

And thus the weary, wearing, endless but interesting days go on. A sort of new Old World will emerge at last, wherein the English will still be dominant and—let us hope—chastened and humbler and, therefore, greater than ever.

Sincerely yours,
WALTER H. PAGE.

To the President

Embassy of the United States of America,
London, June 1, 1916.

DEAR MR. PRESIDENT:

I have periods of great irritation with the English— almost of impatience with them. I suppose that any people would be put on edge by such a strain as this war. But not even such a strain can excuse the foolish flurry that public opinion here is having over one word in your speech to the League to Enforce Peace. You are reported to have said that we are not concerned with the causes or the *objects*[1] of this war. Forgetting all the rest of your speech, the press and the people have singled out the word "objects" and read it to mean that you see no purpose in the conflict, etc., etc., etc. I am sending House a lot of newspaper clippings: I spare *you* such things—except the enclosed letter that Lord Cromer wrote to the *Times*.

My analysis of this whole unhappy incident—for it has its serious as well as its silly side—is this: The German people are getting tired of the war—as who is not? They have been fed on "victories" that were fictitious and especially on the promise of victories that have not been won. Now their loyalty and submission must be fed on

---

[1] On May 27, 1916, President Wilson spoke before the League to Enforce Peace in Washington. In this address he declared that "the United States was not concerned with the causes and objects of the war. The obscure foundations from which its stupendous flood has burst forth we are not interested to search for or to explore." It is doubtful if any of Mr. Wilson's public utterances caused as much pain as this in the Allied counties.

some other diet. The German leaders, therefore, have set going a great peace hubbub: *We* want peace; *we'll* make peace. It's the stupid English, who are whipped, that will not make peace. The continuance of the war, therefore, is wholly the fault of the English and their Allies. Thus, they seek to shift the responsibility for whatever fighting must yet be done off their own shoulders—to save their face to their own people and incidentally to affect neutral opinion. The English, who have received no peace proposal from the Germans and who, Sir Edward Grey recently informed me, have not even discussed peace with their Allies, of course understand this piece of German strategy, are annoyed by it—so annoyed that they have, for a time at least, banished the word "peace" from their vocabulary. A lady said to me to-day: "I no longer use the word: it smells German—as German as *Kultur.*"

It is on this mood that your word "objects" fell; and the anti-American-Government feeling is again all ablaze. Even our best friends of the London press—papers that have hitherto refrained from unfriendly comment—have broken over the censorship and berated us; and all London is talking about the American desire and design to force— or to try to force—peace. Many sections of society and of opinion have worked themselves into an ugly temper.

I am trying, without seeming to pay too much attention to it, to set some corrective influences at work. I am glad to say that the best of the American correspondents here, who are very loyal fellows, are giving their help. I can hardly say, as I wish I could, that this is merely a passing mood. Of course, the subject will presently be changed, but something of this unfortunate mood, I am afraid, will persist.

The serious aspect of it, apart from the gross misreading

of your speech, is that our government is suspect of preferring a premature peace—a peace that would be really a German victory. The English no longer expect a stalemate; they expect a definite result in their favour. They have no foolish idea of driving the German armies to Berlin or of imposing humiliating terms; but they do feel sure of a victory over the German Army and of the complete restoration of Belgium, etc., etc. Just when this expectation has become fixed, he who talks peace talks treason!

Gossip (none of which, so far as I know, has yet got into print) even busies itself with House's visits: "What did he come here for? What message did he bring? He *said* nothing, but he was feeling for peace. We want no peace emissaries. We know ourselves when we shall want peace. The American Government is playing the German game. They don't wish us harm—we know that—but they don't yet even know what the war is about." This is the kind of talk that buzzes everywhere. With House in mind, a questioner asked Sir Edward Grey in the House of Commons yesterday whether the Government meant to send a special diplomatic envoy to Washington. The answer was: "No, His Majesty's Government have complete confidence in its Ambassador to the United States." Thus, this English mood smites everybody on every side.

From this point of observation, the less said about peace, at least till some new and decisive event happen, the better.

All these things and suchlike, though, I take it, you wish to know them, unfortunate as they are, have nothing in them seriously to disturb the philosophic mind. They are, rather, measures of the abnormal effects of the strain of the war. Still, you may be sure that the English mood has reached a fixed determination to spend their last shilling and to send their last man rather than stop before their enemy gives up; and this German peace talk all about the world makes that determination all the stronger. The League to Enforce Peace will have its day, but its day will not come till peace come.

I resolutely refuse to be made the least unhappy by any such outburst of excitement, or the least uncomfortable. The fluctuations of feelings, like the fluctuations of battle, would confuse you if you watch them too minutely; the inevitable result after a while begins to be visible. The inevitable result as regards our relations with the English, will be that they and we will in time become the League to Enforce Peace; and they will thank you, as I now thank you, for showing that when Jefferson spoke of entangling alliances he didn't mean to discourage disentangling alliances.

You wouldn't believe that a three-years' absence and the study all the while of no domestic problem but always of the United States vs. the rest of the world could bring such a mass of ignorance to a man of fair intelligence as my mind now holds about the domestic political condition at home. All my cues are lost. I can't guess what will happen at Chicago next week; but I can't imagine that anything will happen which will put the election in any doubt. All the Americans that I see—and these days they are fewer than at any preceding time for fifty years—hold this opinion. This reminds me, by the way, to say that the resident Americans in London are a right-minded, well-behaved, patriotic group, although of no great importance (a black sheep here and there) who stand up for their country. They are now, for example, quietly and continuously trying to make their English friends understand the indecency of criticizing a speech they haven't read; for only two short paragraphs of what you said have been telegraphed here.

> Yours sincerely and faithfully,
> WALTER H. PAGE.

June 1, 1916.

As I read this letter over, it seems to me unspeakably dull and depressing and most uninterestingly true. I am always, these recent days, swinging from pity and indignation to admiration: the English compel all these emotions and more. I swear at them and I bow low to them. This is not my bowing week. Great Heavens! it's a crazy world—a slaughter house where madness dwells. I keep calm—as calm as one can; and one must keep calm, well balanced, philosophical. That's half the battle.

> W. H. P.

To the President

Embassy of the United States of America,
21 July, 1916, London.

DEAR MR. PRESIDENT:

. . . The following incidents and events confirm or throw some light on these general propositions: As I make it out, there was very little personal sorrow at the loss of Lord Kitchener.[1] This was not only because his intimate friends were few: he had spent most of his life away from home, but the general feeling was that his work was done. Many people, of course, knew too that he was incapable of team work and was a constant and severe trial to his cabinet associates. Yet his death made a profound impression. He had raised the great army— or his name had; and the whole nation roused itself to

---

[1] Lord Kitchener lost his life on H. M. S. *Hampshire*, June 5, 1916.

keep that army in munitions and to do everything else for it. Although the Germans had nothing to do with his death, his death nevertheless acted as an extraordinary stimulus to the war spirit of the whole English nation. You could almost see the grim determination rise in their minds as you see the hot sun raise the mercury in a thermometer.

Sir Edward Grey, who in my judgment is the greatest man in this group here, is so exceedingly considerate of the United States, has such a profound faith in our scheme of things—is so convinced and thorough-going a democrat, practically and idealistically, and so believes in our future —this man will go the whole length that his convictions and his environment will permit to meet our wishes. He has given many proofs of this. But on the particular subjects that directly bear on the conduct of the war he becomes more and more rigid. He has several times almost directly and openly confessed to me that the time has passed when he can always follow his own inclinations. When I find him in the right mood, I linger in his office after my particular business is done and draw him into a general conversation. Standing before his fire (we all had fires during the whole arctic June, and one is burning now in the room where I write) we have gone over schemes of government, the general relations of our two countries, the future of the English-speaking peoples, Wordsworth, fishing (he wrote a book that is a sort of modern Izaak Walton)—any sort of thing that is big and interesting. The other day I went to see him when I had no errand.

"I surprise you," I said, "by bringing you no trouble to-day. I called only to congratulate you on your elevation to the peerage."

He explained the drawbacks. He spoke of the wrench it gave him to leave the House of Commons after thirty years' service without a break, and he spoke with much emotion. He was put in the Lords because Kitchener's successor is a commoner and this makes an unlawful number of Cabinet Ministers in the Commons. Somebody had to become a peer, and for several reasons he is the most suitable and available man. We fell to talking at last about the whole subject of our differences. He remarked that in normal times a democracy takes too little interest in public affairs, but in times of stress it takes too dominating an interest. In normal times, it leaves the politicians too much to their own devices; in excited times it curtails too much their liberty of action. "Why, Mr. Page, if we were to open the door for German reservists to get home from North and South America, in the first place we should commit suicide, and in the second place—I can't say what English opinion in its present mood would do to the Government." There's his confession!

Another remark was this:

"The French Government is much more rigid than we are in construing precedents and international law. Yet their actions do not seem to stir up American resentment as ours do. Is there not in the American democracy a background of old controversies with us about shipping and no such background of any such controversies with the French?"

I couldn't keep from saying, "If that be true, it shows only that the French are luckier in their past than you."

Then he fell to talking about his own future, and this and that; and when I got downstairs where Tom Page[1] was waiting for me, I found him asleep in the automobile! A few nights later Sir Edward dined with me and he gave the whole evening to talk about his eagerness that the

[1]Thomas Nelson Page, at that time American Ambassador to Italy.

United States should not pass severe judgments on the Allies during this life-and-death struggle. Tom Page and another American, just come from home, were here; and I told them to tell him quite frankly what the feeling is in the United States which he had heard from me *ad nauseam*. When they were done he said, "I know it. Now tell me what *I* can do?" He talked of little else to Mrs. Page, who has come to know him quite well and to whom he talks very freely. After the people had gone she said to me: "What's the hitch? It is impossible to believe that Sir Edward does less than he can do to meet our views and wishes. He is a simple, honest, straightforward truthful man. Isn't he?"

"Beyond question," said I.

"Well, what's the matter then—except British public opinion?"

"Very little else. We've got to argue with the whole British people. They've taken the Government, foreign policies and all, in hand."

I think that that is pretty nearly the whole truth.

The matter of our controversies about the mails and about shipping troubles is practically coming more and more into the hands of Lord Robert Cecil, Minister of Blockade, now of Cabinet rank. He is the ablest of the sons of old Lord Salisbury. I think he is the only Tory to the *n*th degree that I ever had a decided liking for. He was the bitterest critic of the Liberal Government, and now under the Coalition he has half his old enemies as bedfellows. I must say that he plays the game squarely. Ugly, gentle, courteous in the extreme, he told me one day that for the present there are only two articles in his working creed: "First and foremost, to win the war and save civilization on the earth, and secondly, to do all that I can to safeguard the rights of neutrals and especially

the United States." And some things he does see, and
he has done some things of practical value. I have had a
long unofficial as well as official fight about the censorship
—of news to the United States, as well as of other things.
I convinced him as I convinced Sir Edward of the desira-
bility of being open and generous to the correspondents of
the American newspapers. Sir Edward agreed with me
but he brought very little to pass; it wasn't quite his job.
But Lord Robert has brought much to pass: he has had
more time. And he has done a good deal to lessen the
delay of the mails. He smooths many little paths. The
broad highways are sometimes too much for him.

He is much interested in "the war after the war," i. e.,
the war of trade. That crusade was conducted here
chiefly by Hughes, the Labour Prime Minister of Australia. Hughes stumped the Kingdom for it. Cities
gave him their Freedom in silver cases. The universities
gave him degrees. The people gave him loud applause.
Half the press hailed him as a Moses. I made a pretty
close study of Hughes. He is not a big man. In many
ways he is an ignorant man. But he is an earnest fellow,
and, I think, quite honest. His economic grasp is not
wide—a somewhat narrow but very earnest and surely
very convincing man, a free-and-easy and ready cam-
paigner with a colonial breeziness which "takes." He
used the background and setting of Australian help and
loyalty with most excellent effect. And he and Lord
Robert Cecil were among the British delegates to the
Paris Economic Conference. Now some things the
Allies will do in "the war after the war." Germans had
used commercial and financial methods in England and
in Russia in particular which were unmoral if not immoral
—methods that might have been taken out of the books
of a decade or so about the Standard Oil Company. They

"dumped" and killed competition by starving out competitors. They conducted systems of commercial espionage, &c., &c., &c. The English were slow to detect these things and sluggish to move against them. They will be neither slow to see nor sluggish to act for some time after the war. They will try, too, to prevent dependence on Germany for dyestuffs and other monopolized articles. These things and suchlike they can and probably will do. No German ships will be allowed to touch here to carry English freight and passengers. Germans will, for a time, find London a hard money market. But the notion of a general Allied Zollverein with preferential tariffs will either never be carried into effect or it will break down so quickly that I am sure nobody need pay much present heed to it. Besides, they will find it impracticable to discriminate against neutrals in any comprehensive scheme. Trade makes its own customs and own laws— in the long run; and no nation is going to cut its own throat—very long. As the whole matter now stands, it is a war measure, a piece of Allied "frightfulness" like German Zeppelins; and it does seem to be annoying the Germans.

The truth is, the mind of this nation now takes in only one subject. Everybody thinks about that and works toward that, in his or her own way, all the time; and that is how to win the war. Nothing else concerns them. All other things seem of so little consequence in comparison that most other things have to wait. The battle in France goes on month after month. Day after day the London papers will contain less than twenty lines of dispatches from the United States, and these have some direct bearing on the war, e.g., the dispatches about the *Deutschland.* The same is true of other neutral countries. It is a time of but one subject for this half of the world. You cannot imagine the depressing monotony of this. Every American who comes here straight from home remarks after a week or less, "I didn't know it was this way. It seemed very different in the United States."

When I went to a camp where there are 3,000 interned (civilian) Germans a few weeks ago and for nearly the whole afternoon heard the complaints of their committees, one doctor struck an original note. "Sir," said he in his most earnest address to me, "the solemn truth is we are all on the road to the madhouse. We've been here, most of us, for nearly two years. We seem or may seem to you to have room enough; we have these grounds to walk and sit in; we do have enough air and space; but I assure you, sir, the monotony of this life is driving us to insanity. There are three men in the hospital now whose brains have gone wrong. I am a physician and I assure you we shall all be mad if we have to stay here much longer." I felt a strong impulse to applaud and to say that he wouldn't find it essentially different outside. . . .

Yet, strange as this paradox is, people are very cheerful. War has come to be the normal state of life: it is not only taken for granted—it gives these people activity that brings in some a sort of exaltation, in many more a form of milder excitement. But the point I have chiefly in mind is the impossibility of inducing anybody to think or to talk about anything else or to consider or to do anything that doesn't seem immediately to help to win it. We are living almost within the sound of the guns of a continuous Gettysburg. I am told that people at certain places on the east coast of England hear the guns distinctly except when the wind is against the sound; and whole trains of wounded and of prisoners are constantly arriving. There is a hospital just through the wall from where I write and another two doors from the building where our offices are. These instances are typical of most of the residential neighbourhoods. A continuous Gettysburg; a tyrannical public opinion; a universal concentration on one subject; an obedient government—to public opinion; a depressing monotony of subject and talk and work, relieved by the exaltation born of a belief in victory—this is the atmosphere we now live in. In the course of time—a long time, I hope—we'll all be on the way to the madhouse.

And the most important news of all is the Department's telegram asking if I think it advisable to go home for a personal conference. I do, decidedly—certainly for my own instruction and benefit. Three years and a half is a long time, especially when two have been war years. Such a visit will be of infinite help to me. Nor do I think that any newspaper sensation can now be made of my going. If leave be granted me, I shall follow this letter a week later. And it will be a great pleasure, as well as a great benefit, to see you, Mr. President.

Sincerely yours,
WALTER H. PAGE.

Soon after writing this letter Page sailed for the United States. The story of that visit has been told elsewhere.[1]

---

[1] See Volume II, Chapter XIX.

CHAPTER XI

ON THE EVE OF WAR

I

THE long-anticipated change in the British Ministry took place in December, 1916. Lloyd George became Prime Minister and Mr. Balfour succeeded Lord Grey as Foreign Secretary. Page's impression of the new Premier appears in the following letter:

To the President

Embassy of the United States of America,
London, 30 December, 1916.

DEAR MR. PRESIDENT:

I made my telegram about Lloyd George so full last night that I have little left to write on that score. The Prime Minister has been ill, the Foreign Secretary has been ill (there's an epidemic of influenza), the Christmas holidays came—so far as any outsider's experience with the new Government goes, they have till now been inaccessible. But so far as any outsider can say, they have made an exceedingly good start. Of course, Lloyd George's enemies predict that he will not last six months. But they are his enemies. His friends and the public in general expect him to finish the war successfully, and (many think) pretty quickly. To me, the new Government seems to promise well—very well. There's a snap about it that the old Government lacked. Lloyd George is not a spent force, but one of the most energetic projectiles

and he methodically tabulates its approaches and maps the shadow that it casts before. I think he would gladly lie down and die to-night to have the horrors of this infernal business ended.

But what I sat down to write you was my belief that Lloyd George will keep the programme that he sketched to me as far as you are willing he should. He will be frank. He is most friendly. He has often expressed his admiration for you—long before he could have known that he would become Prime Minister—and during the year he has shown and expressed to his intimates his confidence in me. He wishes confidentially to use me as a medium to reach you and for you to reach him whenever either of you have need or even an impulse. He is very direct. He does not use circumlocution. He doesn't "intimate": he says things straight out. "Call me on the telephone any time you like," was his parting word. This from the present ruler of the British Empire; for the Prime Minister is of course not only the Chief Executive but the chief and leader also of the House of Commons. I am sure he is quite sincere. Much may come of it, or little may come of it, as you or he will.

This change of government is quite as complete as a change of administration at Washington—when one party goes out and the other comes in. All that I can yet say about it is that it promises well for us.

Yours sincerely,
WALTER H. PAGE.

Memoranda

December 30, 1916.
Written, not for the sake of the gentlemen mentioned, but for possible help to the President and the Service.

HOOVER:

Mr. Herbert C. Hoover, Chairman of the Commission
for Relief in Belgium, would, if opportunity should offer,
make a useful officer in the State Department. He is
probably the only man living who has privately (i.e.,
without holding office) negotiated understandings with
the British, French, German, Dutch, and Belgian governments. He personally knows and has had direct dealings
with these governments, and his transactions with them
have involved several hundred million dollars. He is a
man of very considerable fortune—less than when the
war began, for this relief work has cost him much. He
was approached on behalf of the British Government
with the suggestion that if he would become a British
subject the Government would be pleased to give him
an important executive post and with the hint that if he
succeeded a title might await him. His answer was: "I'll
do what I can for you with pleasure; but I'll be damned if
I'll give up my American citizenship—not on your life!"
Within the last six months two large financial organizations, each independently, have offered him $100,000 a year
to enter their service; and an industrial company offered
him $100,000 "to start with." He declined them all.
When the Belgian relief work recently struck a financial
snag, Hoover by telegraph got the promise of a loan in the
United States to the British and French governments for
Belgian relief of $150,000,000! I do not *know*, but I think
he would be glad to turn his European experience to the
patriotic use of our government. He is forty-two years
old, a graduate of Leland Stanford Jr. University.

LAUGHLIN:

There's nothing in our diplomatic service open to
Laughlin in the way of promotion after he leaves this

till spring he fears that the Germans will make good their threat to sink all ships (including American) that come to England. Hence the extreme desire for peace now.

3

I predict that the President cannot be made to lift a finger for war—until the Germans should actually bombard one of our ports. It's cowardice or pacifism that holds him back every time—Jeffersonianism.

About this time President Wilson's address to the Senate, delivered January 22, 1917, reached the London Embassy. The speech was sent to Page several days before being spoken, in order that he might have it published in full in certain newspapers well known for their pacifist tendencies—such as the *Nation*, the Manchester *Guardian*, and the *Daily News*. This oration represented President Wilson's final appeal for peace. In the main the opinions expressed were just and high minded, and the President's declarations of the principles that should govern the world in future were such as would be echoed by most men of good sense and good spirit. Unfortunately the address contained just one phrase that utterly destroyed its usefulness. Before any attempt could be made to organize a new world order, said President Wilson, it would be necessary to reëstablish peace in Europe. And this must be "a peace without victory." There are probably few Americans to-day who do not regard this phrase as one of the greatest mistakes of President Wilson's career; both those who approve his war policy and those who disapprove are unanimous on this point. The words "peace without victory" implied that, so far as the moral issues were concerned, there was little to choose between the Allies and the Central Powers. The overwhelming triumph of either side to the conflict could represent no gain for mankind. Wilson by implication at least made public acknowledgment that this conception of equal balance was wrong when two months afterward he insisted that the United States should declare war against Germany on the ground "that the world must be saved for democracy." That Page, after considering the import and inevitable effect of these fateful words, should have cabled President Wilson suggesting their omission from his forthcoming speech is only another instance of that farsightedness which he had exhibited from the beginning of the war.

To the President

London
Dated Jan. 20, 1917.
Rec'd 8:50 P. M.

SECRETARY OF STATE,
    Washington.
    5514.   January 20, 1 P. M.
The following is strictly confidential and of immediate importance to the President.

Since there has been an apparent delay in delivering your speech to the Senate I venture respectfully to offer a comment on the phraseology in the sentence about "Peace without victory." My experience of the state of mind in this country makes me fear that unless you define your use of the word "victory" it will be misconstrued as an effort directly to influence the result of the present war, and even as an interference on behalf of Germany, since you took no step while the Germans were gaining military advantages. Any phrase which now appears to the Allies to interfere just when they hope to gain a striking military advantage is enough to provoke a storm

vate concerns in the United States and not our government. But such reminders in no way stopped his rapid talk. He continued:

"If you are drawn into the war I shall be glad for many reasons, but especially because your government will then participate in the conference that concludes peace. I especially desire this because of your President's cool and patient and humane counsel, which will be wholesome for us all."

Then he asked, "Is there any way we can serve you? I have already directed our Army Chief of Staff [Robertson] and the first Sea Lord [Jellicoe] to give you all possible information out of our experience that you may ask for. You will find them communicative to you at any time," and he asked if any other departments of his government could serve us,—"if so come and see me at any time and I will open the way." Perhaps you will send me definite suggestions or instructions on this point.

PAGE.

Two months were to pass, however, before President Wilson took the irrevocable step. They were months filled with exciting events and humiliating moments. During this period Page kept something that resembled a diary; at least he jotted down, now and then, the thoughts that each succeeding crisis inspired. Much as Page welcomed the breach with Germany, and sincere as were his congratulations to the President over that event, the old doubt as to Wilson's constancy still prevailed. The President's reluctant and wavering course as Page regarded it—had left the belief, which he never abandoned, that Mr. Wilson had not understood the issues of the war—or that he persisted in misunderstanding them; that he placed the Allies and the Central Powers on the same moral level; that he looked upon Germany with an indulgent eye; that even after dismissing Bernstorff he sought in every conceivable way to keep the United States out of the war, and that only an overwhelming public sentiment at last forced him into the conflict. After the German declaration of unrestricted warfare American ships kept, for a period, within American harbours. They feared to leave, for they were helpless before submarine attack and knew that they would be torpedoed. The Government itself was unable to afford them any protection. This humiliating situation oppressed Page, as it did all right-thinking Americans and all friends of America in other countries. A law introduced in Congress and supported strongly by President Wilson authorized the arming of American merchant vessels. If they were permitted to carry guns, the captains of these vessels were prepared to run the gauntlet of the submarines; quite properly they declined to do so without such means of defence. This proposed law disclosed an ugly situation in the United States Senate. The purpose was to give American ships a certain protection against the attacks of German submarines, yet a small minority of the upper chamber, led by Senators LaFollette and Stone and assisted by the antiquated Senate rules, used all their ingenuity in efforts to prevent the matter from coming to a vote. Only an amendment to the Senate rules at last enabled the majority to pass the measure. The most sensational episode of this period, however, was the publication on March 1st of a telegram from Dr. Alfred Zimmermann, German Foreign Secretary, to the German Minister in Mexico, outlining a scheme for an alliance of Germany, Japan, and Mexico against the United States, and for the cession, in case of victory, of Texas, New Mexico, and Arizona to Mexico. The hopes, the fears, the uncertainties, the occasional flashes of encouragement and approval that possessed Page's mind in the face of these events are mirrored in his rather haphazard and informal jottings. They are merely the expression of fleeting and varying moods; but the period itself was a variable one; and these paragraphs have a great historic and psychological interest as portraying what was undoubtedly the state of the normal American mind during that great crisis of doubt and of hope. The quickness with which Page notes his approval of the President's acts, when they justify such approval, and the eagerness with which he watches for any sign of positive action, are not their least characteristic features.

February 25, 1917.

It is a momentous time. First, *the submarine menace:* The submarines are destroying shipping at an appalling rate. The percentage of lost ships—of all the ships afloat—is small, of course; and the hopeful men are always reminding us how small it is. This, to give comfort to the population. But there is a menace, nevertheless—a very grave menace. The small number of ships that can carry food—that can be spared from war uses— makes this percentage-comfort smaller than it seems. On the other hand, nobody knows, outside the Admiralty, how fast the Navy is capturing or destroying the submarines. After all, everything depends on this latter fact. The hope that I get is, since the Navy has twice overcome vigorous submarine attacks, they are likely to overcome this one. True, the Germans now have more submarines, larger ones and stronger; but the Navy has had corresponding experience. But food may be lacking in the meantime.

In the meantime, too, *American ships* keep port. For some reason our government will not arm our ships or permit them to be armed; and they are keeping their docks. We are practically blockaded—held up, held in, driven off the seas by the German threat!

The Germans on 22 February sank *seven Dutch* ships. Thus, the *submarine menace* is very real; and there is much fear. Read Lloyd George's speech in the papers of two days ago about food restriction, production, etc., etc.

Then the military situation now, just before the severe fighting can be begun in France. The soldiers are all hopeful. General Sir Douglas Haig's famous interview a week ago with a French journalist predicts a clear victory. All the military men feel very sure. But there was a note of doubt through a large part of civilian life; the German Army is still very large—how strong, it remains to be seen. Awful carnage awaits us in any event—awful, awful, awful.

It is an anxious time.

(While Stevens is sketching me!)

Tuesday, February 27, 1917.

The President's Speech to Congress yesterday asking for authority and credit to establish "armed neutrality" is published and received without much comment in morning papers. It distresses **W. A. W. P.**[1] Laughlin is pleased.

"Admirable," he says. Looked at over a considerable period the President's course has progressed—slowly, perhaps, but steadily—from neutrality (hard and severe), to warning, to a break in diplomatic relations, to "armed

[1] Mrs. W. H. Page.

neutrality." Apparently there is only one step more
possible. Or can there be any intermediate step?

About the time the President was delivering that
speech news reached us and Washington of the torpedoing
of the *Laconia* and the death of Mrs. and Miss Hoy, of
Chicago. What effect will this have? An "overt act"
surely.

Mr. Hoy, son and brother of the dead women called—
greatly wrought up—will wire President—will join United
States Army if we go to war, or British Army if we do not
—an able, determined-looking fellow of thirty-six. Frost
at Queenstown has made very good reports indeed on the
Laconia—no German apology in any dispatch. I am
asking official statement from Admiralty.

A letter from A. W. P.[1] is full of fire and ginger—not
enough leadership for him.

Lord Grey of Fallodon writes me an excellent letter;
it'll be a black page in American history if America sits
still after six or seven Dutch boats have been sunk.
(He hadn't heard of the *Laconia*.) He proposes that
United States silently convoy American and neutral
ships and see if Germany dares sink one or to sink a convoy.

More than a billion pounds of new money in the War
Loan! That's impressive, surely.

Friday, March 2, 1917.

It would be hard to imagine a more rapid succession of
exciting events, and yet we refuse to be excited! Startling
things have become normal. The Zimmermann (Berlin)
Mexican-Japan bomb burst to-day, the Zimmermann
telegram to the German Minister in Mexico being in the

[1]Arthur W. Page.

morning papers. They gave it out in Washington (apparently) to cause Congress to give the President authority to arm merchant ships, &c., &c., as he should see fit, and to use the armed forces of the nation to protect commerce and life. It had that effect. An enormous majority in the House last night (nearly 500 to 13!) voted in favour of the resolution. I am curious to see the effect on the country. I have never abandoned the belief that if the President were really to lead, all the people would follow. Whether he will even now lead remains to be seen.

Yesterday I told Chinda, the Japanese Ambassador, about this Zimmermann telegram. He thought it a huge joke at first. To-day Yates Thompson confessed that it seemed to him a newspaper hoax! Nobody (few people surely) yet thoroughly understands the German. This telegram will go some distance surely to instruct the people of the U. S. A.

The danger is that with all the authority he wants (short of a formal declaration of war) the President will again wait, wait, wait—till an American liner be torpedoed! Or till an attack is made on our coast by a German submarine!

Many members of Congress and others in Washington do not yet believe the authenticity of this [Zimmermann] telegram. Hence the Department telegraphed to-day for the *German* of the translation, which I sent them. Now they have Bernstorff's code message, the German of it and the English of it. See the London papers' editorials.

Mr. Balfour, Mr. Bonar Law, and I to-day had a conference of an hour or more about exchange with the United States and the possibility of more loans there to pay for munitions and food bought there. Could a great popular loan be got in United States (like the great

blot in history or a failure that must grievously depress the future history of America."

PAGE.

13 March, 1917 (Tuesday).

It's well to be patient in judgment, surely.   Hard on the President's tame and vague inaugural and his apparent wandering off into the by-way of a controversy with the Senate—hard on these came a few days ago a definite announcement that American ships will be armed fore and aft and that other ships, armed, will be admitted to our ports!   And an Extra Session of Congress is called for April 16th.[1]   Now that's the stuff!

Meantime, not only the Zimmermann Note to the German Minister in Mexico has done its work on public opinion, but there have come to light various German intrigues, for example, to get Colombia and Nicaragua to get into a row with the United States.   Look out for the Canal!   Then the practical certainty looms on the horizon of submarine bases somewhere in Central America.

Hence a complete reversal of the Government's position about admitting armed merchantmen.   Hence a complete (almost complete) cessation of trade quarrels with Great Britain, such as filled the whole sky when I was in Washington last autumn!   Even the President was full of indignation at the British Government for these atrocious crimes.   Nobody saw or would believe that the Germans stirred up all this, then!

Curious coincidence: Bernstorff reached land in Norway on the very day Gerard reached Havana!

Bagdad fell on Sunday—the end of the German Eastern dream, for the English are not likely to give that up.

To-day I spoke at the unveiling (in St. Paul's) of a

---

[1] An error; Congress met on April 2.

tablet to the memory of E. A. Abbey, H. R. H. the Princess Louise pulling the string. I took Mrs. Abbey to and from the Cathedral.

Unless Germany modifies her submarine plan and exempts all American ships, we shall now soon have war —unless peace come by an almost sudden collapse, which hardly seems likely. Well, we must go in, when we go in, "with both feet."

At Colefax's at dinner last night, Colefax and Sir George Askwith *et al.* speculated on whether Lloyd George will last as Premier till the war ends. The underhand intrigue that almost every group and party indulge in— Good Lord! deliver us! The Dardanelles Report was published (as the Asquith old Cabinet think) in order to discredit them. It *has* discredited them, whether that were the purpose or not.

20th March, 1917.

The Russian Revolution holds the attention, engages the speculation, and fills the newspapers.

As for American things—the three American ships, news of whose sinking came on Saturday, seem really to have stirred the people to a mood that may possibly cause them to run over the President. Everybody is now fearful lest, if we "get into the war," we'll get in with only one foot—will go submarine chasing, and when the British Navy has driven the submarines home, we'll quit war—*à la* Vera Cruz, and the expedition to catch Villa. That, however, can hardly be if Germany *declares* war on us—which she may not do, because of this very hope.

We haven't broken with Austria yet.—Peace?—

But our ships (American merchantmen) are coming with **guns and gunners.**

subsequent events disclosed, looked not unfavourably upon this ambitious proposal, was the same Carranza whom President Wilson had supported for the Mexican Presidency among a multitude of revolutionary candidates. Carranza was President of Mexico, indeed, as the result of a succession of events that amounted almost to American intervention.

Page at once transmitted this information to the State Department:

To the President

London,
Dated Feb. 24, 1917.
Rec'd 9 A. M.'

SECRETARY OF STATE
Washington.
5746, February 24, 2 A. M.
In about three hours I shall send a telegram of great importance to the President and Secretary of State.

PAGE.

To the President

London,
Dated February 24, 1917.
Rec'd 8:30 P. M.

SECRETARY OF STATE,
Washington.
5747.   February 24 1 P. M.
My 5746, February 24 8 P. M.
Confidental for the President and the Secretary of State.
Balfour has handed me the text of a cipher telegram from Zimmermann, German Secretary of State for Foreign Affairs, to the German Minister to Mexico, which was sent via Washington and relayed by Bernstorff on January

19th. You can probably obtain a copy of the text relayed by Bernstorff from the cable office in Washington. The first group is the number of the telegram, one hundred and thirty, and the second is thirteen thousand and forty-two, indicating the number of the code used. The last group but two is ninety-seven thousand five hundred and fifty-six, which is Zimmermann's signature. I shall send you by mail a copy of the cipher text and of the decode into German, and meanwhile I give you the English translation as follows:

"We intend to begin on the first of February unrestricted submarine warfare. We shall endeavour in spite of this to keep the United States of America neutral. In the event of this not succeeding, we make Mexico a proposal of alliance on the following basis: make war together, make peace together, generous financial support and an understanding on our part that Mexico is to reconquer the lost territory in Texas, New Mexico, and Arizona. The settlement in detail is left to you. You will inform the President [that is, President Carranza of Mexico] of the above most secretly as soon as the outbreak of war with the United States of America is certain and add the suggestion that he should, on his own initiative, invite Japan to immediate adherence and at the same time mediate between Japan and ourselves. Please call the President's attention to the fact that the ruthless employment of our submarines now offers the prospect of compelling England in a few months to make peace.

(Signed) ZIMMERMANN."

The receipt of this information has so greatly exercised the British Government that they have lost no time in communicating it to me to transmit to you, in order that our government may be able without delay to make

years had had continual access to their most confidential information. This German confidence in their Intelligence methods cost them dear. Relying upon the secrecy of their codes, they developed an amazing telegraphic loquacity in the course of the war. They were constantly filling the atmosphere with the most intimate news of their Navy, Army, and their Diplomatic Service, and all this information the British were quietly taking out of the ether and quickly deciphering. The result was that the British Government had as accurate information about everything German as the Germans themselves. The movement of every German submarine was about as well known to the British as it was to the German Admiralty; every time one left a German port the British had an accurate record of that fact; they followed its voyage day by day, and even plotted it on the map. Similarly, as soon as any message involving any department of the German Government was entrusted to wireless, the British promptly seized it and reduced it to understandable English.

On the 16th of January, 1917, the ever-watchful ears of the British wireless operators detected the characteristic spluttering which informed them that another German message was speeding through the air. When decoded, the British found that they possessed this somewhat disjointed but still extremely valuable document:

Zimmermann to Bernstorff for Eckhardt

W. 158,
16th January, 1917.

Most secret for Your Excellency's personal information and to be handed on to the Imperial Minister in ? Mexico with . . . by a safe route.

Tel. No. 1

We propose to begin on the 1st February unrestricted submarine warfare. In doing so, however, we shall endeavour to keep America neutral . . . ? If we should not [succeed in doing so] we propose to [? Mexico] an alliance upon the following basis:

(joint) conduct of the war

(joint) conclusion of peace.

Your Excellency should for the present inform the President secretly [that we expect] war with the U. S. A. [possibly] [. . . Japan] and at the same time to negotiate between us and Japan . . . [Indecipherable sentence meaning please tell the President] that . . . our submarines . . . will compel England to peace in a few months. Acknowledge receipt.

ZIMMERMANN.

This somewhat confused message gives an idea of the difficulty of picking up wireless symbols sent across the Atlantic—at that time—in midwinter. But there is a conspicuous discrepancy between this telegram and the more complete and finished one sent to Bernstorff by way of the Washington cable office and by him relayed to the City of Mexico. The plan for dismembering the United States and making President Carranza a free gift of Texas, New Mexico, and Arizona does not appear in it. Whether this omission was the result of defective wireless work or has another explanation is not yet clear.

Evidently Herr Zimmermann still feared that his instructions to Eckhardt would not reach their destination, for this very painstaking Foreign Secretary sent them by a third route. In the British Admiralty this Nauen-Sayville thoroughfare was known as the "main line"; it was the most direct and consequently the one most used for sending German dispatches to the United States.

But the Foreign Office had another way of communicating with its Ambassador in Washington. The extent to which Swedish diplomatic agents were transmitting German messages constituted one of the gravest scandals of the war. That the Swedish Foreign Office was so used is now no secret; in fact, the American Government itself disclosed the part Sweden was playing, when, in the summer of 1917, it published the notorious "sink without a trace" messages of the German Minister at Buenos Aires. The fact seems to be that the Swedish Court was openly pro-German; that popular opinion in Sweden similarly inclined to the German side; and, by January, 1917, the Swedish Foreign Office had become almost an integral part of the German organization. In many capitals German messages were frequently put in Swedish cipher and sent to Swedish Ministers in other countries and by them delivered to their German colleagues. Herr Zimmermann, in his desire to make certain that his Mexican telegram should reach Washington again fell back upon the assistance of his Swedish confrères. He handed his message to the Swedish Minister to Berlin; this functionary sent it to Stockholm, Sweden from this point it was cabled to Buenos Aires, Argentina and from that city cabled in turn to Washington. The journey was a roundabout one, covering about ten thousand miles. Yet nothing that was sent through the air or under the sea seemed to escape the watchful attention of the British Naval Intelligence, and this Swedish message was captured almost at the same moment as that one which was going by the "main line."

The German Government forwarded this dispatch to Washington in still another way. Indeed, the most remarkable incident in this remarkable transaction remains to be told. Evidently the German Foreign Office feared

that transmission by wireless and cable transmission to
Buenos Aires—by grace of the Swedish Government—
might fail them.   The prohibition the American Government had placed upon the use of wireless from Nauen
to Sayville, Long Island, might naturally cause apprehension as to the delivery of messages sent by this route.
The cable line from Stockholm to Buenos Aires and
thence to Washington and Mexico was a round-about
one and a message transmitted that way might con-
ceivably fail to reach its destination.   The dispatch of
this telegram, however, was at that moment the most
important business before the German Foreign Office, and
its safe arrival in the City of Mexico must be assured at
any cost.   There was one method that was absolutely
certain, though the fact that this should have occurred to
Zimmermann must be regarded as one of the most auda-
cious and even reckless strokes of the war.   Humour of any
kind the Germans seldom displayed at crises of this sort,
yet the mechanism adopted to make certain that this plot
against the American people would safely land on Bernstorff's desk evinces an unmistakable gift—even though
an unconscious one—for the sardonic.   The transaction
reflects so seriously upon the methods of the State Department that it would probably never have seen the light
had the Germans not made it public themselves.   In
1919–20 the German Constituent Assembly held an elab-
orate investigation into the responsibility for the war.
In this the Zimmermann telegram played its part.   Among
its published documents is a note which reveals one route
by which this document found its way across the Atlantic.[1]
It says: "Instructions to Minister v. Eckhardt were to be

---

[1]See Vol. II, p. 1337, "Official German Documents Relating to the World War.
Translated under the supervision of the Carnegie Endowment for International
Peace, Division of International Law."

taken by letter by way of Washington by U-Boat on the 15th of January; since the U-Boat *Deutschland* did not start on her outward trip, these instructions were attached on January 16 to telegram No. 157, and through the offices of the American Embassy in Berlin telegraphed to Count Bernstorff by way of the State Department in Washington."

What this means is that the German Foreign Office used the American Government as an errand boy for the transmission of a document that contained a plot against its own territorial integrity. The coolness with which Bernstorff sent his financial accounts to the German Foreign Office in the American diplomatic pouch—documents that contained the details of his propaganda work at Washington—has already been set forth.[1] The use of the American State Department in transmitting the Zimmermann telegram is another instance of a similar kind. The German Government, many times in the course of the war, used the good offices of the American State Department for transmitting messages to Ambassador Bernstorff. Germany had no cable communication with the United States, the wireless was unreliable and not always available, occasionally therefore the Germans would request Washington to serve in this capacity. As all such messages touched England before starting across the Atlantic the consent of the British Government was necessary before the favour could be performed. That the British graciously permitted the Germans to use their cable facilities may possibly have seemed, at the time, an act savouring of the magnanimous; the fact, however, that the British possessed the German cipher and read all these messages as they sped through England creates the suspicion that they may have regarded this as a way of

---

[1]See ante, page 274.

obtaining valuable information. From the American standpoint, however, the proceeding was without precedent. Ambassador Gerard, of course, is not subject to criticism, as he merely carried out the explicit orders of his Government. But it is a well-established principle that no government, especially in war time, ever transmits the dispatches or official documents of another without knowing what they are. No government ever makes such a request without submitting the contents of such official papers. Had the usual procedure been adopted, Germany would have handed its messages to the American Embassy in Berlin, which would have enciphered them into the American code and transmitted them to Washington. Unless Germany were willing to do this, the administration of course should have declined to act as the intermediary. The very fact that the Germans were unwilling to submit to this usual method in itself was a sufficient proof that the proffered document was one our Government could not send. That the Germans went to the extreme of using the State Department as a medium for sending such information to Bernstorff certainly discloses a contempt not flattering to American vanity; yet that Zimmermann should have used a route one of whose stopping places was English soil shows that he himself was almost as simple as he believed Washington to be.

At this time President Wilson was practically his own Secretary of State, and these German messages were sent on his explicit orders. There are reasons to believe that the State Department itself disapproved the whole transaction. The procedure in the Zimmermann matter is especially illuminating. According to the German official statement, already quoted, this telegram was attached to another, No. 157, for the transmission of which the German Government had obtained the Presidential con-

sent.   The only information vouchsafed about this latter
message was that it pertained to the "peace efforts" on
which Mr. Wilson was then engaged.   It did indeed refer
to those peace endeavours, but in a most indirect fashion.
In it the German Foreign Office informed Bernstorff that
the German Government "promises the early termination
of the war and the restoration of that peace which the
President has so much at heart"—and that it proposed to
bring about this result by the institution of unrestricted
submarine warfare.   Message "No. 157," in other words,
was Germany's official notification to its Ambassador in
Washington that it had decided to take the fateful step
which brought the United States into the war.   This
message was sent January 16th, and in it Bernstorff was
instructed not to notify Washington until the first of
February.   The Zimmermann telegram was attached;
the whole document was put into the German cipher and
handed to Mr. Gerard.   Mr. Gerard telegraphed it to
Copenhagen, thence it went to London, thence to the
State Department at Washington and there was delivered
by the State Department to Bernstorff.   In London, of
course, the Intelligence Service seized it and rendered it
into comprehensible English.

Almost as soon as this communication was sent,
therefore, the British Government acquired possession
of it in four ways.   It was "bought" in Mexico.   It
was picked up in the wireless route from Nauen to Sayville.   It was intercepted on its way from Stockholm,
Sweden, to Buenos Aires.   It was sent by the American
State Department—and also intercepted.   Important as
was the information that it contained of a Germanic
attempt to secure a Mexican-Japanese alliance against the
United States, the telegram and accompanying messages

concealed another piece of information which was almost as startling. The first sentence declared that "we propose to begin unrestricted submarine warfare on February 1st." The date of this message is January 16th—practically two weeks before Count Bernstorff made this announcement to the American authorities.

Both President Wilson and the State Department wished to give this Zimmermann telegram to the press. The President had sent Bernstorff home; relations with Germany had been severed; there seemed every likelihood that this act would result in war; this telegram, disclosing Germany's plot for the invasion by Mexicans of the United States and the dismemberment of American territory, would enormously strengthen the President's hand. Moreover, the President saw that this evidence of Teutonic intrigue would exert an important influence in a section of the country which, in his opinion, was not enthusiastic for war. The Middle Western and the Southwestern States would now discover that German aggression might concern them more intimately than they had previously suspected. They would find that the Kaiser, in the event of success, was planning to deliver large sections of their own region to Mexico.

Evidently the State Department wasted no time in locating the telegram in the Washington cable office. There it was discovered, just as Page had informed the President that it would be. The Administration itself, of course, had no suspicion that it was not authentic, but it foresaw that this question would arise. It wished to be able to assure the American public that it possessed the message and had deciphered it. Page was therefore asked if the British could not send the German code to Washington for this purpose:

To the Secretary of State

London,
Dated March 1, 1917,
Rec'd March 2, 12:30 A. M.

SECRETARY OF STATE,
Washington.
March 1, 11 P. M.
Your 4493, February 28, 8 P. M.

CONFIDENTIAL. . . . The question of our having a copy of the code has been taken up, but there appear to be serious difficulties. I am told actual code would be of no use to us as it was never used straight, but with a great number of variations which are known to only one or two experts here. They cannot be spared to go to America. If you will send me copies of B's[1] cipher telegrams the British authorities will gladly decipher them as quickly as possible, giving me copies as fast as deciphered. I could telegraph texts or summaries in matters of importance and send the others by pouch. Neither Spring Rice nor Gaunt[2] knows anything about this matter.

PAGE.

The matter was easily arranged, for Mr. Edward Bell, Secretary of Embassy in charge of Intelligence, was extremely close to the British Intelligence Service. The Zimmermann telegram, as uncovered in the Washington cable office, was sent to Mr. Bell. The British lent him their precious German code, and Mr. Bell in a few hours deciphered it. Thus Mr. Wilson could assure the American people, when the time came, of its absolute authenticity. The President insisted also that he should have it in the

---

[1]Obviously meaning Bernstorff.
[2]British Naval Attaché at Washington.

original German.   The results of Mr. Bell's work are embodied in the following message.

To the Secretary of State

London,
Dated March 2, 1917,
Rec'd 10:45 P. M.

Secretary of State,
    Washington.
    5789.   March 2, 4 P. M.
My 5784 of to-day.   Bell took the cipher text of the German messages contained in your 4494 of yesterday to the Admiralty and there, himself, deciphered it from the German code which is in the Admiralty's possession. The first group, 130, indicates Bernstorff's number of telegram number . . .   The second group, 13042, indicates the code to be used in deciphering the cipher telegram.   From the third group onwards, message reads as follows:

"Auswaertiges Amt telegraphiert Januar 16: No. I Ganz geheim selbst zu entziffern.   Wir beabsichtigen am ersten Februar uneingeschraenkt U-Boot Krieg zu beginnen.   Es wird versucht werden Vereinigte Staaten von Amerika trotzdem neutral zu erhalten.   Fuer den Fall dass dies nicht gelingen sollte schlagen wir Mexico auf folgender Grundlage Buendnis vor; Gemeinsam Krieg fuehren. Friedenschluss.   Reichlich finanzielle Unterstuetzung und Einverstaendnis unsererseits dass Mexico in Texas, New Mexico, Arizona frueher verlorenes Gebiet zurueck erobert.   Regelung im einzelnen Euer Hochwohlgeboren ueberlassen.   Sie wollen vorstehendes dem Praesidenten streng geheim eroeffnen, sobald Kriegsausbruch mit Vereinigten Staaten feststeht und Anregung hinzufuegen

ment had disclosed that denials would be useless. Zimmermann knew that a Germanic disavowal would be followed by the production of the Bernstorff telegram discovered in a Washington telegraph office; instead of denying, therefore, the German Foreign Office undertook to explain.

President Wilson wished to quiet the detractors by publishing the German text, but the British had good reasons for not wishing this done.

To the Secretary of State

London,
Dated March 10, 1917,
Rec'd 5:30 P. M.

SECRETARY OF STATE,
Washington.
5822, March 10, noon.
4516, March 8, 4 P. M.

The authorities directly concerned would prefer that the German text should not be published, as its publication in entirety would indicate that our Government or some other parties are able to decipher the German code used in its transmission from Washington to Mexico and the Germans would then cease using it elsewhere. This is information which, judging by Zimmermann's reported statements, they do not now possess and a confirmation of what they may suspect would be of great value to them. At present the Germans cannot know exactly where or how the leak occurred; for all they know a copy of the message may have been lost or removed from the German Embassy in Washington, or the leak might have occurred between Berlin and Washington.

Were serious doubts being cast in America on the genuineness of the instructions to the German Minister in Mexico the authorities here might reconsider their position, but as Zimmermann has admitted their genuineness in the Reichstag this can scarcely be the case.

PAGE.

Had Zimmermann made this denial, he would probably have been embarrassed by a sheaf of other telegrams dealing with his frustrated statesmanship. After Bernstorff's dismissal by the United States, the Wilhelmstrasse became active once more. The Mexican Alliance appeared more desirable, as the probability of war with America increased.

Zimmermann to Eckhardt[1]

To Mexico
No. 11
8th Feb., 1917.

In continuation of No. 1.[2]

Most secret. Decipher personally. Provided there is no danger of secret being betrayed to U. S. A. you are desired without further delay to broach the question of an alliance to the President. The definite conclusion of an alliance, however, is dependent on outbreak of war between Germany and U. S. A. The President [President Carranza of Mexico] might even now, on his own account, sound Japan.

If the President declines from fear of subsequent revenge, you are empowered to offer him a definitive alliance after conclusion of peace, provided Mexico succeeds in drawing Japan into the Alliance.

ZIMMERMANN.

[1] German Minister in Mexico.

[2] The original message of January 16th, published above.

ments of the Entente will continue to have confidence in Japan's loyalty and its determination to extend all possible aid and share the difficulties and hardships until the struggle against Germany and cruelties ends."

Baron Shidehara, Vice-Minister of Foreign Affairs in Japan, said in a statement to the Associated Press, "We are greatly surprised to hear of the German proposal. We cannot imagine what Germany is thinking about to conceive that she could possibly involve us in war with the United States merely by asking Mexico. This is too ridiculous for words. Needless to say, Japan remains faithful to the Allies."

A message of March 7th reveals the anxiety that was growing in Berlin:

Zimmermann to Eckhardt

From: Berlin   No. 16,
To: Mexico   7th March, 1917.

Please burn compromising instructions. Entirely approve your attitude. We have openly acknowledged cable Dispatch No. 1.[1] In connection with this, emphasize that instructions were only to be carried out after Declaration of War by America.

Cable Dispatch No. 11[2] is of course being kept strictly secret here also.

(Signed) ZIMMERMANN.

Evidently the negotiations with Carranza had not ceased, however, for the question of supplying the Mexican army was a pressing one:

---

[1] The original Zimmermann telegram of January 16, 1917.

[2] To Mexico. No. 11 of 8th February: "You are desired without further delay to broach the question of an alliance."

Zimmermann to Eckhardt

From: Berlin   No. 17,
To: Mexico   17th March, 1917.
Reply to Telegram 7.[1]

Find out what kind of munitions and arms are wanted and to what Mexican port on East or West Coast a German ship [under] foreign flag could proceed.

Mexico must procure arms so far as possible from Japan and South America.

But the German Foreign Office was not resting all its hopes upon Carranza. It could use his bitterest enemies in Mexican politics for its own purposes.

Mexico-German Military Attaché to Berlin

March 24th, 1917.

Vice-Consul at Mazatlán reports that Villa, aided by Germans, is expecting to receive three cargoes of munitions by sailing vessels to be landed between Mazatlán and Manzanillo. Cantu[2] is believed to be conniving.

Vice-Consul states this information is trustworthy.
Addressed to Washington.

On April 6th the American Congress declared the existence of a state of war with Germany. The German correspondence with Mexico clearly proves that the arrangement for an alliance was making rapid progress. A message of April 13th is sufficient:

---

[1] From Mexico of 26th February: "Could WE provide arms and ammunition?"
[2] Another Mexican revolutionary leader. His field of operations was Lower California.

element of comedy; and this the Germans, all unconsciously, now proceeded to supply. Astonished as were Americans and Englishmen when this Zimmermann telegram was made public on March 1st, the Imperial Government was more astonished still. The curiosity that was manifested in England and the United States as to the manner in which the leak had taken place was even more acutely felt in the Wilhelmstrasse. In all countries plenty of explanations were forthcoming. All of these paid Americans the compliment of assuming that they were responsible for the discovery—a misapprehension which both governments intended to disseminate. Especially amusing phases of the sensation were the attacks made in the British press upon their own inefficient Government; how inferior the British secret service was to the American! Every newspaper reporter on this side of the water explained the mystery in a way of his own. The one which seemed to be the most plausible was that the telegram had been found among Count Bernstorff's effects when his baggage was overhauled at Halifax. A circumstantial story was printed describing how American soldiers had captured Bernstorff's messenger on the Mexican border and found the incriminating evidence on his person.

The interest of the German Foreign Office in this great mystery took the form of many telegraphic messages which now passed back and forth across the Atlantic—all of which, like the original telegram itself, the British intercepted, deciphered, and placed permanently upon the record. These were passed around at the time among a select few in the American Embassy and the British Foreign Office and were the occasion of much hilarity. Page, with his alert sense of fun and with his well-known love of everything German, found these telegraphic manifestations of Teutonic woe an endless delight. Probably the most agitated man at that time in the German diplomatic service was Von Eckhardt, the German Minister in Mexico, who promptly saw in the newspaper accounts of March 1st the end of his diplomatic career, and who, with a lamentable lack of sportsmanship, proceeded to fix the blame upon his colleague at Washington.

Eckhardt to Zimmermann

From: Mexico   No. 8,
To: Berlin   March 1st, 1917.

The newspaper here, the *Universal*, which is friendly to the Allies, publishes to-day exactly the same information as yesterday's Washington telegram, ostensibly as having been in President Wilson's hands since the breach of relations, the text of cable Dispatch A, No. 1. Of course I did not make the communication here. Treachery or indiscretion here out of the question; therefore apparently it happened in the U. S. A., or cipher 13040 is compromised.

Cable Dispatch No. 11,[1] which was forwarded to me by the other known way, has so far not been published.

I denied everything here.

VON ECKHARDT.

But Berlin desired more explicit information:

Stumm to Eckhardt

To: Mexico   No. 20,
                            21st March, 1917.

MOST SECRET. DECIPHER PERSONALLY

Please cable in same cipher who deciphered Cable Dispatches 1 and 11, how the originals and decodes

---

[1] The message of February 8th enjoining him to take up negotiations immediately for the alliance.

were kept, and, in particular, whether both dispatches were kept in the same place.

STUMM.[1]

The German Foreign Office apparently had no intention of letting Von Eckhardt off too easily. It persisted in believing that the trouble had all started in Mexico City:

Berlin to Eckhardt

From: Berlin   No. 22,
To: Mexico   27th March, 1917.

Various indications suggest that the treachery was committed in Mexico.

The greatest caution is indicated.

Burn all compromising material.

This message evidently greatly disturbed Von Eckhardt, for he now gives impressive details, including additional evidence that Bernstorff's organization is guilty:

Eckhardt to Zimmermann

From: Mexico
To: Berlin   27th March, 1917.

Both dispatches were deciphered, in accordance with my special instructions, by Magnus. Both, as is the case with everything of a politically secret nature, were kept from the knowledge of the Chancery officials.

Telegram No. 1 was received here in cipher 13040, while Kinkel,[2] who is at present employed here, thinks he remembers that it was sent off by the Washington Embassy, like all telegrams sent here in cipher, from Cape Cod.[3]

---

[1] Of the German Foreign Office in Berlin.

[2] Formerly an employé at the German Embassy in Washington.

[3] Where there was a cable station.

The originals in both cases were burned by Magnus and the ashes scattered. Both dispatches were kept in an absolutely secure steel safe, procured especially for the purpose and installed in the Chancery building, in Magnus's bedroom, up to the time when they were burned.

Reply to Tel. 21 Order carried out. Cable Dispatch No. 18 is still missing.

With a view to making preparations for the period after the war, I suggest if possible the immediate appointment of Herr Lubeck—compare report No. 69 of 3d November —as Commercial Adviser to the Embassy.

ECKHARDT.

Eckhardt to Zimmermann

From: Mexico   No. 14,
To: Berlin   30.3.17.

Reply to Telegram No. 22. Greater caution than is always exercised here would be impossible. The text of telegrams which have arrived is read to me at night in my dwelling house by Magnus, in a low voice. My servant, who does not understand German, sleeps in an annex. Apart from this, the text is never anywhere but in Magnus's hand or in the steel safe, the method of opening which is known only to him and myself.

According to Kinkel, in Washington even secret telegrams were known to the whole Chancery. Two copies were regularly made for the Embassy records. Here there can be no question of carbon copies or waste paper.

Please inform me at once, as soon as we are exculpated, as we doubtless shall be; otherwise, I insist, as does Magnus also, on a judicial investigation, if necessary, by Consul Grunow.

With ref. to Tel. No. 11, Director Schmidt of the

Deutsche Bank, New York, has telegraphed to Lima that the probability of an American loan to Mexico was increasing.

(Signed) ECKHARDT.

This was too much. The "low voice," the "steel safe," the "scattered ashes," and non-German-speaking servant were evidently accepted by Berlin as complete exculpations of Von Eckhardt, who presently was delighted by the following telegram, giving him a clean bill of health:

Foreign Office to Eckhardt

From: Berlin   No. 28,
To: Mexico   4.4.17.

After your telegram it is hardly conceivable that betrayal took place in Mexico. In face of it the indications which point in that direction lose their force. No blame rests on either you or Magnus.

FOREIGN OFFICE.

The humour of the situation, of course, resides in the fact that both Bernstorff and Von Eckhardt were responsible, for the message was uncovered both in Mexico City and Washington.

Who was mainly responsible for unearthing the Zimmermann telegram? The work was done by the Intelligence Service of the British Admiralty. The head of that department was Admiral William Reginald Hall, a man not widely known in the United States, but one to whom this country has every reason for profound gratitude. The part that Admiral Hall played in the war is vividly told by Page in a letter to the President:

To the President

London, March 17, 1918.

DEAR MR. PRESIDENT:

. . . Hall is one genius that the war has developed. Neither in fiction nor in fact can you find any such man to match him. Of the wonderful things that I know he has done, there are several that it would take an exciting volume to tell. The man is a genius—a clear case of genius. All other secret service men are amateurs by comparison. If there be any life left me after this war and if Hall's abnormal activity and ingenuity have not caused him to be translated, I wish to spend a week with him in some quiet place and then spend a year in writing out what he will have told me. That's the shortest cut to immortality for him and for me that has yet occurred to me. I shall never meet another man like him: that were too much to expect.

And (whether it becomes me to say so or not) Bell and I have his complete confidence and that fact entitles us to some special consideration in the esteem of our friends. For Hall can look through you and see the very muscular movements of your immortal soul while he is talking to you. Such eyes as the man has! My Lord! I do study these men here most diligently who have this vast and appalling War-Job. There are most uncommon creatures among them—men about whom our great-grandchildren will read in their school histories; but, of them all, the most extraordinary is this naval officer—of whom, probably, they'll never hear. He locks up certain documents "not to be opened till 20 years after this date." I've made up my mind to live twenty years more. I shall be present at the opening of that safe.

For his great achievements, Admiral Hall was made a Knight Commander of St. Michael and St. George by a grateful Government. The record is appropriately concluded by the correspondence that passed between him and Page and Colonel House:

Page to Sir William Reginald Hall

American Embassy, London,
October 24, 1917.

DEAR SIR WILLIAM:

I have waited, perhaps ungracefully, to send you my congratulations on your K. C. M. G., because, once having you in range, I wished to take a double shot at you. I am sincerely glad, not only at this honour done you because you have so richly deserved it, but also because it was bestowed on you not in a long list of other honours, but all by itself on you alone. I think I see in this unusual fact a special significance. None of your many friends rejoice more truly than we who dwell and labour at the sign of this Embassy, which is most grateful to you.

And now I have the additional pleasure, under instructions sent to me directly by the President, to convey his personal thanks to you. I quote from his letter:

"You will at an early time take some private occasion to assure Admiral Hall of my very great appreciation of what he has done and of the spirit in which he has done it."

May I add an expression of my great personal gratification at being instructed to convey this message to you?

I am,

Yours most sincerely,
WALTER H. PAGE.

Sir William Reginald Hall to Page

25 October, 1917.

MY DEAR AMBASSADOR:

I find it difficult to say how very much I appreciate your most kind letter, which has touched me deeply. I do assure you that nothing has given me more pleasure than the work which I have had the privilege of doing with you and your Embassy, and I shall ever feel grateful to you for the singular kindness you have shown to me. It will always be, as you may well imagine, a lasting memory and gratification to me that at a time when your great nation was taking a decision which affected the civilization of the whole world you honoured me with your confidence.

I don't know how to thank you for the kind words in which you convey the President's personal message.

I venture to ask that, should you be writing to the President, you would say to him that in honouring me with his words of warm appreciation, I feel that I have received the very highest reward, and that I shall always treasure his message as one of my most valued possessions.

I am, my dear Ambassador,
Very sincerely yours,
W. R. HALL.

Edward M. House to Sir William Reginald Hall

115 East 53rd Street,
New York.

REAR ADMIRAL HALL,
The Admiralty, London.

DEAR ADMIRAL HALL:

I want to congratulate you and felicitate you over the great work you have been doing.

I believe you were largely responsible for the overthrow

of the recent German Ministry—certainly Zimmermann's downfall was brought about by the exposé of his note to the German Ambassador in Mexico.

I cannot think at the moment of any man who has done more useful service in this war than you, and I salute you.

Sincerely yours,
E. M. House.

September 22, 1917.

CHAPTER XIII

PRESIDENT WILSON'S ATTEMPT TO DETACH AUSTRIA FROM GERMANY

ON April 2d President Wilson asked Congress to declare that a state of war existed between the United States and Germany. On April 6th the two nations were at war.

To the President

London, April 17, 1917.

SECRETARY OF STATE,
Washington.

6018, April 17, 3 P. M. Confidential for the President. The King summoned me to Windsor Castle to spend last night and gave me a private audience of more than an hour, and talked with me again at some length after dinner. He is most appreciative of our help which he very frankly confessed is much needed. He hoped the naval, military, and technical men of both countries will so fully and frankly confer as to prevent our repeating British mistakes. The most serious submarine situation, the dire need of ships, and the fear lest Russia make a separate peace were his chief topics. He expressed high appreciation of Admiral Sims's visit and spoke of Mr. Balfour's mission,[1] for which I thanked him. He remarked: "I do not know how Balfour can now be spared, but nothing else is so important as giving your government all the information we have." He feels content with the present military situation in France, but he is much con-

[1]To the United States. See Volume II, Chapter XXII.

cerned, as everybody here is, who knows the facts, about the submarine warfare. He spoke with the greatest appreciation of your last speech in Congress and of your leadership.

He added: "People are talking much about absolute monarchs; there is no monarch, thank God, in Europe who has the power of the President."

His conversation throughout was full of appreciation.

PAGE.

Why did President Wilson let two months elapse between the dismissal of Bernstorff and the declaration of war against Germany? One reason for the President's delay appears in an important letter written Mr. Wilson on February 22d. The President was attempting to detach Austria-Hungary from the Germanic Alliance and cause that empire to make peace. The United States did not sever diplomatic relations with Austria-Hungary when it gave Count Bernstorff his passports; and in fact this country did not declare war against the Dual Monarchy until December, 1917. Just what the effect would have been had Austria-Hungary separated from Germany in February, following the American break, is conjectural; it might have been extremely important; indeed, there was a probability that such a development in itself might have brought the European war to an end. One possible outcome would have been the shifting of the Italian Army to the western front—though this is doubtful; at least it would have made unnecessary British and French activities in Italy, and the energies of the British Navy in Mediterranean waters could have been transferred to the area south and west of Ireland. This in itself would have been a great gain. The elimination of Austria would have meant the speedy collapse of Bulgaria and Turkey, for these nations, their communications with Germany severed, would have been helpless and a speedy prey to the Allies. This would have ended the favourite Pan-German "Mittel-Europa" scheme, and destroyed the long-cherished dream of a Germanic empire extending from the North Sea to the Persian Gulf. The separation of Austria-Hungary from Germany, could it have been accomplished at that time, would have been a great achievement, and the plan naturally enlisted the hearty coöperation of Page. There was, of course, practically no chance that it could succeed. Italy was an insurmountable obstacle. The terms she would demand of Austria would be terms that Austria, desperate as was her condition at that time, could hardly be expected to grant. But the incident has great interest, if for nothing else for the light which it sheds upon the methods and the temperament of Mr. Lloyd George.

The proposal at first was not cordially received by the Prime Minister. Page has left this record of his first conversation on the subject:

He demurred at once. No; if Austria-Hungary make peace that will open blockade on the South; we shall have to grant her more than we wish to grant, etc., etc.,—all rapidly, like a machine-gun. And he asked me for the present not to mention the subject to any one, not even to any member of his Cabinet.

To the President

American Embassy, London.
22 February, 1917.

DEAR MR. PRESIDENT:

I telegraphed so fully about my interviews with Lloyd George concerning a possible Austrian peace proposal that

I need write only certain minor illuminative incidents. At my first interview I expressed my astonishment at his conclusion—that Austria was a greater hindrance to Germany as an ally than she would be as a neutral. To my arguments he simply repeated his conclusion—with amazing rapidity. The most hopeful thing that I could then induce him to say was that he would take some of his associates into his confidence and tell me when there was anything more to say. But on top of this he forbade me to mention the subject to any members of the Government "for the present." That for the time being balked me. It was as if an Ambassador at Washington had taken up a subject with you, had got your answer, and had asked leave to discuss it with members of your cabinet. If you had said "No," he would of course have been silenced on the penalty of forfeiting your confidence, if he had gone further. It occurred to me, then, that perhaps I had made a mistake in going to him first. Yet any other course would have been discourteous to him after his request that I should take up with him informal subjects of high importance; for he is practically Dictator. All that was left me to do was to pursue him relentlessly since I could pursue nobody else—or to give it up; and I had no idea of resting with the answer he had given me.

The very next day I had what seemed a piece of good luck. I was invited by a member of the Government to dinner a few evenings later—"the Prime Minister will come." After dinner I talked again with Lloyd George. "Nothing to say further yet," he said. "I haven't had a chance to go over the subject with the men I had in mind." Then I got up a little dinner myself for him, to which I invited the Jellicoes, the Bryces, and several other couples of high degree. Again I asked him, "What news?" He shook his head. I took him aside and remarked on the ease with which great men and great governments make great mistakes. Lloyd George is perhaps the easiest man to talk with (not necessarily to convince) of all men that hold high places. He has little dignity. He has no presence, except as an orator. He swears familiarly on easy occasion. But he has as quick a mind and as ready speech as any man that I ever encountered. It is impossible to realize that his casual deliverances are the Voice of the British Empire. After more talk, in which he had injected an oath or two, I made bold to say, "Good God! Prime Minister, have you forgotten that the whole object of the war is to reduce Europe to peace, and here may be peace that you are rejecting—how do you know?" But I got no satisfactory response. This was my third interview.

I still refused to believe that this was to be the end of the matter. Now, queer accidents happen when you keep steadily on one quest and see many people and hear much talk; and by an accident I found out that Curzon[1] was opposed to discussing peace with anybody and had talked with the Prime Minister, and that Jellicoe was eager for peace with Austria and had not been able to talk with the Prime Minister on the subject. That very night I dined with Lord Salisbury. Lady Curzon was there—without Lord Curzon. Lady Curzon, married just a month, began life as an Alabama girl, and you can yet distinguish the Alabama intonations in her speech as you now and then hear the oboe in an orchestra.

"Where's your husband?" I asked her.

"He had to spend the evening with the Prime Minister." That sounded somewhat discouraging.

The next day was Sunday. I recalled that Admiral Jellicoe left his ceaseless watch at the Admiralty every

[1] At this time Lord Curzon was Lord President of the Council.

Sunday afternoon at five o'clock and went home to meet his friends at tea. At five o'clock, therefore, Mrs. Page and I were there to pay our respects. I could not yet mention the subject to the Admiral, but I gave him a chance to mention it to me. Not a word did he say about it. He told me only that fishing (for submarines) was pretty good—that's all.

A full week had passed and I had got no further than I had got at my first interview. I resolved to go and see the Prime Minister again at his office. I rehearsed my arguments, which seemed to me irrefutable, and I was determined to fight to the last ditch. To my surprise, he yielded at once—gracefully, easily, almost unbidden. He had somewhat modified his views, he said—provided —provided the greatest secrecy could be maintained. By this emphasis he gave me the cue to his thought and mood.

The German proposal of a peace conference a little while ago, which, because no terms were named, was regarded by the British as a trick, steeled the nation and the Government in particular against all peace talk till the spring campaign and the submarine war decide something. The very word "peace" was banished from the English vocabulary. Lloyd George himself in several speeches had declared that there could yet be no peace— no thought of peace. This was his state of mind when I first brought up the subject and the state of mind of the nation. Peace men had been hooted in the House of Commons and suspected peace meetings had been dispersed by the police. His emphasis on secrecy made his fear plain. No doubt if he could announce Austria's surrender that would be a great stroke. But if it got abroad that he were "dickering" with Austria or anybody else about peace, he would lose his Dictatorship overnight. He was afraid of the subject. But having discussed this particular possibility of eliminating Austria with some of his colleagues, he "had somewhat changed his view."

I feel the necessity to be on my guard with Lloyd George. Perhaps I do him wrong. Of course, his political enemies (and he has many and fierce enemies) say that he is tricky and untruthful. They are not good witnesses; no doubt their judgment is unfair. But he is changeable—mercurial. He reaches quick conclusions by his emotions as well as by his reason—he reasons with his emotions. He has been called the illiterate Prime Minister, "because he never reads or writes." He is the one public man in the Kingdom who has an undoubted touch of genius. He has also the defects of genius. He has vision and imagination, and his imagination at times runs away with him. That's the reason he's the most interesting man here—an amazing spectacle to watch. He compels admiration and permits, but does not compel, complete confidence. I wish I instinctively had the same unquestioning and unshakable confidence in him that I have in Edward Grey, whose genius is all the genius of character. A Scotch friend of Lloyd George was defending him the other night in a little group of men who expressed fear of his emotional adventures, and one of them asked about his truthfulness. "Oh, he's truthful—perfectly truthful. But a Scotsman's truth is a straight line. A Welshman's is more or less of a curve." But how this Kingdom has waked up under his leadership! There's something ramshackle and slipshod about him and his ways and his thought. But he has organized England, man power, pound power, mind power, will power, as perhaps no man ever did before.

The situation, therefore, so far as the mood of this

Government is concerned, is just as good as it would
have been if the Prime Minister had given the answer we
wanted when I first brought the subject to him—only a
week was lost because of this extraordinary man's extraordinary mood and of his extraordinary attitude to me
whereby he had me bound to secrecy on pain of becoming
a traitor to him; and his extraordinary attitude to me
comes of his admiration for you and from his wish to have
you at the conference that will make peace.

Now, of course, I have talked with others. Mr. Balfour
is eager to see a proposal from Austria, provided he can
believe it to be a genuine proposal. He and others have
some fear of the hand of Germany in it—fear that it may
be a trick. But the answer that the Prime Minister gave
me at my last interview is the answer of the Government.
They will give thorough and appreciative attention to any
proposal that comes.

Very heartily yours,
WALTER H. PAGE.

Additional details appear in several entries in Page's
memorandum book:

I made an engagement to call on the Prime Minister
(Lloyd George) at 3:15. To prevent the newspapers from
discovering my visit I walked to Downing Street and
came up the steps at the end of the street, and I sent
my car to wait for me at the steps of the German Embassy.

I renewed my conversation with the Prime Minister
about receiving formally the offer of peace (if the President
can send it now) of Austria-Hungary. The President
(said I) is keeping relations with Austria-Hungary open
with the hope of doing this great service. Have you

anything to add to what you previously said? I then put the case as strongly as I could.

"It would be a good thing to detach Austria," said he.

Whew! He had said just the contrary a little more than a week ago! Curzon, I suspect, had talked with him before my other interview, and he had conferred with somebody else. I brought him to definiteness—at first, he was a little reluctant. But he finally committed himself fully.

As I walked away from Downing Street this reflection occurred to me: I sat down and talked to this Dictator of the British Empire as calmly and as easily as if I had gone to see a man on some trifling errand—to order a pair of shoes, to engage a room at a hotel, or any other commonplace errand. I stated the case earnestly but precisely as I would have stated any commonplace case to any man. He was still a little reluctant—he feared publicity. Would it be possible to let *him* alone see it?—No; the President wished to present it formally. He yielded—all in a commonplace way. We two men were talking about and trying to devise a plan for ending the war—surely a subject to excite anybody. There was no excitement—only a commonplace argument and at last a favourable response.

"Thank you; good-day."

"Good-day."

I fancy that all great transactions and conferences are done so. The momentousness of such occasions comes afterwards—is a sort of afterthought.

I fear that if the Austrian peace inquiry were now to come again, all the members of the Government would take the view of it which the Prime Minister took at first—that it was a mere German trick. As mild and temperate and just a man as Mr. Balfour said to me privately a little while ago: "I have the greatest admiration for the President, as you know; but I am afraid (and I do not wonder at it) that he does not yet know the German Government. It is an incredible thing. We did not know it either. If the President had known it he would never have addressed the European neutrals as he did when he broke relations with Germany. These neutrals are simply terrorized. They dare not speak out. Germany could and would smash Denmark and reduce her to ruins—as she did Belgium, Poland, and Serbia—she'd smash Denmark in a week and Holland in a month. She sinks their ships wholesale and drowns their crews till their ships have practically been taken off the seas. And what can they do? They are, in fact, already conquered but not destroyed."

CHAPTER XIV

"ON THE BRINK OF THE PRECIPICE"

THERE is a certain satisfaction and interest in recalling now the heartening effect upon the Allied cause produced by the American declaration of war. Just how desperate the situation was appears from a group of letters written in the summer and autumn of 1917. Over and over Page records his belief, and the belief of all the leaders in the Allied countries, that only American intervention had prevented an Allied defeat, or at least an inconclusive and humiliating peace.

To the President

June 8, 1917, London.

DEAR MR. PRESIDENT:

The liveliest satisfaction has of course been felt here at the way in which the registration of men under the conscription act went off. For two days it has been a chief topic of conversation everywhere. But this convincing and dramatic demonstration of our people's earnestness was not needed to make all thoughtful men here understand: they understood already. Our ready supply of large sums of money, the prompt coming of our destroyers and Admiral Sims, and now the coming of General Pershing, and Mr. Balfour's reception had done the work. The English appreciation is genuine, profound, and complete. The story is told about London of a deaf and half-blind old countess who had been a very great lady in her day—that, when someone told her that the United States had come in, she asked,

"Come into what?"

"Into the war."

Then she said, "Well, my dear, the subject doesn't interest me in the least."

I have heard of no other such deaf and blind person. The expressions of gratitude by all classes and on all sides are touching and continuous. In St. Paul's the other day an American legion of the Canadian Army brought an American and a Canadian flag to be blessed and to be deposited in the Cathedral till the end of the war. In the special prayers written for this service were two for the divine guidance of the President and people of the United States, and nothing would do but for Mrs. Page to take part in the ceremony by passing our flag from the donors to the Bishop. They work the poor lady and me in so many touching duties that we have composed a prayer of our own for protection against being worn out. The King asked me to present to him the first of our units of doctors and nurses. When another unit of nurses, on a sight-seeing tour, went to St. Paul's one day, they were met at the door by "a most engaging and well-informed clergyman," who spent hours in showing them everything. They accidentally discovered as they were coming away that he was "The Very Reverend and Honourable the Lord Bishop of London," who had come five miles to have the pleasure of meeting them. When I next saw him, he said: "Noble women whom God has sent in our extremity!" Although he is a fighting Bishop, his eyes were damp. I could write you a volume of such incidents. A group of our nurses were walking on the street and they met a dignified old Englishman. He pulled off his hat and bowed and said, "God bless you, ladies." The

Canon of Westminster asked the privilege of himself showing one group through the Abbey. An old man who has a
fine country place twenty miles from London asked another group to spend Sunday with him. He had all our
patriotic airs played, and a photographer took the group
on his lawn, he among them; and he remarked, "This for
posterity. This is an immortal event."

Admiral Sims is the darling of the Kingdom. The Admiralty regards him and treats him as if he were one of
their own admirals. The Admiral[1] (British) at Queenstown is going on a fortnight's vacation and he has asked
the Admiralty to put Sims in command there of both
British and American fleets during his absence. He has
made a great personal as well as professional impression.
Among the most popular shows of the war is the film pic-
turing the arrival of our destroyers, and admiring stories
about our young naval officers constantly make their way
from Ireland.

General Pershing comes to-day. The Government calls
me in to ask whether they shall give him a government
dinner. My reply was that General Pershing is come
to fight and not to dine; we are all in to win the war. "Help
us on this errand first. Then, if there be time, we'll dine.
Yet—also give him a dinner now, for the effect it will have
at home. It will please our public to see that your
hospitality and good feeling and appreciation are in good
working order." So the dinner is on. Of course I also
am giving him a dinner to meet the high military authorities and the Prime Minister.

It may please you to know that the Government
consults me about everything, from small things like a
dinner to things of great importance, asking, "How will
this be received in the United States?" The King asked

[1] Sir Lewis Bayly.

about his receiving the Admiral; now about his receiving the General. The secretaries in the Embassy have a joke among themselves—that the Ambassador has become a Member of the Government without portfolio. I have made several of the secretaries members of government committees—on Blockade and the like—at the Government's request. So far as I can see they are playing the game openly and squarely and opening all doors to us. The hinges on some of the doors are yet a little rusty, but they are shining them up.

The prompt passage of the conscription act opened their eyes to our earnestness and efficiency more than any other single event.

While, of course, the Government is giving all its thought and attention to the conduct of the war, there is a constantly growing discussion of possible peace, and especially of economic arrangements to follow the war. Nobody sees peace or any near chance for it. But thoughtful men constantly discuss the possible advisability of making Trieste and Salonika "internationalized" ports so that the Balkan States may have free access to the Mediterranean. Everybody foresees the terrific difficulty that will arise in trying to apply any general principle in the Balkans—this on the assumption that the Allies win a decisive victory—give the Germans a complete thrashing. And trade after the war fills increasing space in print and in discussion, with no concrete result so far. But this topic is now worked very hard as a military weapon—for effect during the war. The British theory is that if Germany can be made to see that practically the whole world will discriminate against her trade after the war, she will be the more likely to give in at some early time. For this reason much emphasis is laid here on

Brazil, and for this reason hopes are entertained that China may come in.

By the way, it will please you to know that the British press and people have clearly seen the great influence on Central and South America of the policy of the United States toward these sister republics; and they applaud your management of this matter.

In fact, they understand us far better in every way than they ever did before; and they understand *you*.   In half-a-dozen groups of men lately the conversation has turned (a favourite topic) on what personalities will emerge largest from the war.   Somebody always remarks, "You mean *after* the American President?"   And the discussion starts on that basis.

I still maintain that the attitude (the changed and changing attitude) of the English is the most interesting subject in the world and—in the long run—the most important.   It is very difficult to describe it.   I have twice tried in letters to you that seemed too unsatisfactory to send.   Take certain facts like these: The first discussion of sensible and appreciative plans for really popular education—the education of all the people—ever heard in this Kingdom is now beginning; and the head of the Government Chemical Research Bureau, in discussing with Professor Hulett the work of German chemists, remarked, "It isn't the Germans we are afraid of, it's you Americans";—take these facts (and I could put down 300 such), you can't help seeing and feeling the ground-swell influence of the United States as the strongest pull on this English planet that it has ever been subjected to; *and they know it.* If Europe is to be made even reasonably safe, it'll be only through our help; *and they know it.* I heard an Australian general tell an old peer that if the

British Empire didn't make a proper place in Imperial Government for the great Colonies, Australia would see if she couldn't join the American Union! The English are waking up to see the vast burden of useless *impedimenta* they carry. All interesting things follow from this.

The studies that all these subjects open—enticing and fascinating and absorbing and necessary studies—I have been trying with my staff to make, at least in some fashion. Mr. Buckler[1] is working in what time he can get on the Balkan situation; he and I together are looking up and keeping tabulated all that seems worth while about peace terms and proposals and possibilities and the feelings and hopes of men worth while. And we have other such studies going. There are of course always many interesting conversations on these subjects. We have equipped a dining room in the basement of one of our office buildings where we have luncheon served (at our personal expense) and we have anybody there from Ministers and Admirals down, out of whom we wish to get information. With high sailors and soldiers and statesmen and writers of books thus to help us, we are trying to pack ourselves and this Embassy as full as we can.

Meantime, praise God, our destroyers are making the approach to these shores appreciably safer, General Pershing is now in conference with the Big British Generals, our doctors and nurses have been going to France for a fortnight (you would be thrilled to see the important English people who have flocked to my house to meet them), and gratitude to the United States beams on every countenance we meet.

Yours very faithfully,
WALTER H. PAGE.

---

[1] William H. Buckler, Special Attaché at the London Embassy.

To the President

London, 22 June, 1917.

DEAR MR. PRESIDENT:

Problems of organization press for larger and permanent coöperation with the British. I have telegraphed about the War Conferences which the European Allies have held from time to time. The next Conference will come about the middle of July. Mr. Balfour thinks, and I think, that our Government ought to be represented. The Prime Minister, the Foreign Secretary, and the War Minister will probably attend it, with a General as a military expert. The larger policies regarding the conduct of the war are considered. Incidentally, these Conferences bring to light the incredible friction between the Allies and their apparently irreconcilable differences. It is not a happy family. For instance, the Italian Prime Minister, I hear on good authority, has already served notice that his Government will not be represented at the next Conference if peace with Austria is to be discussed. Here comes the everlasting question of boundaries. Italy opposed to the last the deposition of King Constantine. A communication that I am sending to the Department from the Greek Minister here, by the instruction of his Government, throws light on the Italian attitude. Then, too, there is the perpetual and baneful Trade-Union of Monarchs. Almost every country that has a king is opposed to the deposition of any king. The Tsar, the King of Spain, the King of Italy, and presumably Queen Alexandra, at least, of England, who is Constantine's aunt, used their influence to the utmost to save him. These cross-currents of dynasties, the special ambitions for territory of practically every continental Ally, which of course conflict, the commitments of England herself to some of them made to get them or to keep them in the war—all these make such a tangle as to defy logical adjustment; and underneath the surface a quarrel is always imminent. When Lloyd George told me this morning that any effort to make a separate peace with Austria-Hungary or Bulgaria was premature because it seemed wise to wait and to see whether Russia will fight again, he did not know that I knew of Italy's unwillingness to discuss peace with Austria; and if Italy is unwilling to discuss peace with Austria, she is unwilling, of course, to discuss peace with Bulgaria. Lloyd George gave me one reason—no doubt a good one, but there was also another and stronger reason in his mind.

Perhaps we ought to be represented at these Conferences, if for no other reason, to get a clear insight into these strong controversies and differences under the surface. To judge only from such as have come, and as are constantly coming to my knowledge, they are numerous and exceedingly embarrassing.

Some weeks ago there was a more or less general fear here lest France herself might say, "Well, I've almost exhausted myself; I can go no further. Great Britain must carry on the war." The coming in of the United States gave her new spirit and new hope. This accounts in some measure for the extraordinary display of sentiment when General Pershing reached Paris—I cannot say how much cold truth there is in this quite generally held British opinion. But I do know that it had much to do with their profound appreciation of our help.

Again—the friction between the Australians and Canadians and the British sometimes reaches seriousness. There is likely to be a stiff controversy when the lid is lifted.

Many such seamy-side pieces of information come to

me, but only as reflected and refracted by English minds.
I imagine we ought to learn them—such as are true—
authoritatively. I get them by sometimes eating three
meals a day and committing other such intimacies with
the men who have attended these Conferences.

Regarding the establishment of a military mission here
—that seems necessary and urgent. Men, committees,
commissions come, some bringing credentials from some
department of our Government and some bringing none;
and in not a few cases several of them seek the same
information that was given to their predecessors a week
or two weeks ago. Then they go away. In a few more
weeks new information is acquired and nobody gets that.
This whole business of our Government seeking information from this Government ought to be systematized
and coördinated. Officers of our Government of technical
training ought to remain here—most of the subjects dealt
with are military—and inquiries should be made of this
commission by all branches of our Government, and all
inquirers should come to them. About this, too, I have
telegraphed. The principal Allied governments have
just such a practical working arrangement. I have
telegraphed about this, too.

The British views that reach me in army circles are as
cheerful and hopeful as the news that comes from navy
sources is discouraging. There is no danger of a serious
shortage of food for any period that may be foreseen.
But the generally informed fear a very serious lack
of such materials as oils, steel, copper, etc., for uses both
for the fleet and for the army. There is no doubt of a very
grave fear raised by the submarines. The Admiralty is
dejected. No submarine "antidote" has been found.
A few are sunk. But there are vast armies that must
yet be killed before the Germans will *have* to give in. The

feeling here is that if the submarine success were discouragingly diminished, the spirit of the German Army would quickly fail.

The multitudinous tasks of preparation in the United States reported, but reported very briefly, in the London papers, make a most favourable impression, and these reports are read here most gratefully. In their gratitude there is a confession of the Allies' dire need of our help—a far more urgent need than anybody confesses or than anybody realizes but the men who know the inside facts. I have had momentary fears that the British may depend on us too much and expect too much—a state of mind that, however much we do, will lead to disappointment. But there is yet no evidence of this. And I am glad to say I have yet seen no evidence to show that the British will "lie down on us"—relax their efforts because we are now helping. They are not built that way. They have vices and they are not always easy to live with or to fight and die with and we shall have our troubles with them. But I do not expect them to try to put their own tasks on us. Their continental allies have depended too much on British help, and the British have keenly felt the unfairness of being too heavily leant on.

In fact, nothing could keep these nations all together a week but dire necessity: it's another case of all hanging together or all hanging separately.

Two facts mark the successful progress of the war: the fall of kings—all thrones are unsteadier; and the steady fall of the mark. Its decline was greatly accelerated by our coming into the war. This decline is a measure of the judgment of the world on the struggle.

Northcliffe's[1] errand is causing criticism here, which was inevitable. He has many bitter enemies, being a

---

[1] In June Lord Northcliffe came to the United States as head of a British mission.

stimulating and contentious fellow. He has done good service in many (perhaps most) of his crusades; for most of them have been directed against more or less incompetent men. He indulges in crusades rather than criticism. But I think the criticism of him has now spent itself. And since he has no diplomatic authority and is a business man of extraordinary ability and energy, I think his appointment a good one. Our Government may deal with him very frankly. He is the friendliest of Englishmen to us. His papers have all been singularly fair to us. He knows and likes the United States, and it is very well worth our while to show our appreciation of his friendliness and helpfulness. Any attention that you yourself may show him will bear good fruit. He is perhaps the most powerful man now living in Great Britain—how much by reason of and how much in spite of his methods, it would be hard to say. For the twenty years that I have known him he has done our country steady and useful service in his vast influence on British opinion. . . .

Sincerely yours,
WALTER H. PAGE.

To the President

American Embassy, London,
14 August, 1917.

MY DEAR MR. PRESIDENT:

No suggestion or proposal has been received here with a heartier welcome than your proposal to send Admiral Mayo and other naval officers for a conference here about the naval situation. Mr. Balfour welcomed it eagerly and the Admiralty is equally pleased. I ought to add that Admiral Sims, too, is particularly pleased.

Since the war began the Admiralty has of course hoped that the German fleet would come out for a fight. The

Jutland battle was a bitter disappointment because it was not conclusive; and since then, as before, the British naval programme has been defensive. The Admiralty opinion, which, as I understand, is unanimous among naval officers, is that the German naval bases (in Germany) are impregnable. Mines, submarines, and the biggest concealed guns in the world are supposed to make any sea attack a foolhardy failure. In front the Germans have Heligoland and they have an open back door into the Baltic.

I don't know how sound this reasoning is; but I do know that its soundness has at every stage of the war been questioned—somewhat timidly, but still questioned. There has been an undercurrent of doubt. The several changes that have been made in the personnel of the Admiralty have seemed to have a thought of some change of the defensive programme in mind. The one method of attack that one ever hears discussed openly is by aircraft. For that, the British have never had enough machines to spare. Moreover, it seems to be too far from the German naval bases to any British aircraft base, unless seaplanes can be used from the North Sea.

But there seems to be no doubt of the open-mindedness of the Government to any suggestion.

The most pressing naval question—the most pressing question of the whole war—continues to be the submarines. They have found no "antidote." The "mystery" ships catch a few—I do not know how many, but not enough to discourage the Germans. A few more are destroyed by other methods; but the problem of catching them at their exit is unsolved. They make their way along the territorial waters of Denmark and Holland and come out to sea wherever they find it safe. I have gone over many maps, charts, and diagrams on which the presence of submarines in British waters and at sea is indicated; and the one thing that seems to be conclusively proved is that the convoy is the best means so far put into practice to increase safety. The future of the world seems to me to hang on the answer to this question: Can the war be won in spite of the submarines? Can a great American army be brought over and its large subsequent supply fleet be sufficiently safeguarded? As matters now go, three large British ships are sunk a day. How many are sunk of other nationalities, I do not know. At this rate, the Allies can hold out long enough to win provided our armies and supplies can come over—convoyed, of course—with reasonable safety. But in the course of time the present rate of ship destruction will greatly weaken the Allied endurance.

British opinion is that the war must be won on the battlefield—that the German armies must be beaten by arms and by economic pressure in Germany; that the German naval bases are untakeable; that the submarines must be endured. And it is universally understood that American intervention is all that saved or can save the Allied cause. France will be practically exhausted by the end of this year as an offensive power; Italy counts for little except to keep a certain number of Austrian troops engaged; Russia, as a fighting force, probably will not recover in time. The probability that is generally accepted is that the war, unless Germany collapse during the next six months by reason of economic exhaustion or by the falling away of Austria or Turkey or both, will become a war between Germany and the English-speaking nations, all which except the United States are already partially exhausted.

The waste in the war caused by the failures of the European allies to work together with complete unity is one of the most pitiful aspects of the conflict. The recently begun offensive by the British on the northern French coast, now interrupted for the moment by heavy rains, ought to have been undertaken long ago. But the French withheld their consent because (so the British military authorities say) a certain section of French opinion feared, or pretended to fear, that the British would keep these coast towns and cities if they were permitted to retake them from the Germans! It is reported, too, that the Belgians objected. The Belgian Army now holds 3,000 yards of the whole trench line: that's all; and the British have so little confidence in them that they keep all the time in easy reach enough reserves to hold this 3,000 yards if the Germans should attack it. This jealousy and distrust run more or less through all the dealings of the continental allies with one another. It's a sad tale.

Yours sincerely,
WALTER H. PAGE.

To the President

London, September 3, 1917.

DEAR MR. PRESIDENT:

. . . Some time ago, in a general conversation, Mr. Balfour said something like this to me: "There is universal admiration and wonder at the American energy and earnestness in getting into the war, which has no parallel. But there are people who privately express a certain fear lest your ardour may cool with the first wave of war-weariness. What should one say to them? Mind you, I have no such fear myself, but I am sometimes met with the necessity to allay it in weaker minds."

I replied: "To put it in good American, the real answer to any such person is, 'Go to hell!' But the judicious answer is, 'Who is going to cool American ardour and how will he go about it? The dam is burst and the flood is come. Will you do me the favour to refer all such persons to me?'" I haven't seen any such yet. But such a fear, which I have no doubt was felt in ignorant quarters, is forever laid by your letter to the Pope. And the leadership of the war is now definitely and confessedly transferred to you, in British opinion.

The acknowledgment of this took many forms even before this letter. Several of your speeches, notably your speech asking for a declaration of war, have been reprinted in dozens of forms for wide distribution. There's hardly a reading household in the Kingdom but has a copy.

. . . The telegrams and other documents, telegraphed to you, which show the customary insincerity and cold-blooded willingness to murder, touching the Argentine Republic, it is here hoped, will, if you have published them, bring the Argentine Government into the war. It is hoped, too, that the proof of Sweden's using her Ministers and pouches in Germany's behalf may cause a change of government in Sweden.[1] The smuggling that has been done through Sweden is the most helpful to Germany of all her channels of supply; and the large quantity of iron ore that has gone from Swedish mines is, perhaps, the most valuable help from outside that Germany has got since the war began.

Admiral Mayo's coming has given the whole Government and especially the Admiralty great satisfaction. As soon as he came I invited the chief Admiralty officers and British Admirals to dinner to meet him, and they have shown him continuous attention since. He told me to-day

---

[1] In early September Secretary Lansing published a series of telegrams sent by Count Luxburg, German Minister in Buenos Aires, containing instructions to German submarine commanders. The phrase "sink without a trace" gave these messages a particular infamy. They were sent in Swedish code through the Swedish Legation in Buenos Aires.

that they are showing him everything that he cares to see and are answering all his questions. The Naval Conference (British, French, Italian, and American) begins to-morrow. Immediately after the Conference ends, Admiral Mayo will visit the Grand Fleet. The submarine activity continues (as I regard it) to be a most serious thing. Convoyed ships have come safely, which seems to point to success in our getting troops and supplies to France. But the toll that the submarines continue to take of unconvoyed freight ships is making the trouble of shipping very great. All ships will have to be convoyed.

This Government is most anxious for a number of our Representatives and Senators to make a visit to England and France, not really for any specific legislative conference, although the invitation may take that form, but for personal interchanges of experience. It is a common saying in England that even no Englishman can really understand the war and its problems who has not made a visit to France. I recall that I was forcibly struck with Bryce's confession to this effect, after he had come back from France. It is on this principle—that it is well for American legislators to get as vivid an idea as possible —that the British are eager for a number of them to come. I agree with them.

The abandonment of Riga, it is feared here, will mean the German occupation of Petrograd, and that will mean the getting of more supplies from Russia and the getting of men, too, for all sorts of labour—will mean, in fact, the prolongation of the war. The German spirit, in spite of hunger, can be kept up by such a land victory and by the continued submarine success for Heaven knows how long; and these German successes seem to point to the slow and murderous necessity of whipping the German Army, lock, stock, and barrel. That, with our help, is only a question of time. But within that time the sickening loss of life will continue. But for the falling down of Russia and the psychological effect of the submarine campaign I should have a very lively hope of the German collapse before the coming winter is gone. The public and the Government here set high expectations on your embargo.

Take your actions all together—from the Conscription Act to the embargo—what a record that is! Of course, it has saved the Allied cause, which would otherwise have been lost, in great measure if not wholly. And the British know that and freely say so. This in itself is a conquest over British "arrogance" which makes us henceforth the masters of the English-speaking world.

Lord Reading again goes to the United States—on the ship that carries this. He goes on a general financial errand, the details of which I do not know—further than the necessity of coming to some concrete understanding. So far as I can find out, the British use their money well (allowing, of course, for the waste of war from which every nation suffers); but they seem to me to be awkward and careless and then suddenly panic-stricken in their large dealings with us to procure money. The financial conferences to which they have invited me seemed to me like a voyage through mist till you suddenly come to a great fall. I have prayed them to be definite before they become panic-stricken. "The Ambassador is quite right," exclaims the Prime Minister. We then adjourn till the next scare comes; and then the same journey is taken again—to the same Nowhere.

Yours very faithfully,
WALTER H. PAGE.

Serious as the submarine situation was, there was another matter that, in Mr. Balfour's eyes, was even more alarming; that was the condition of Allied finances. That the Allies were seriously pressed for dollars to cover their purchases in the United States is no secret. Yet the expressions which British statesmen used, in conversation with Page and in their own official papers, are fairly startling. On June 28th Page was asked to meet Mr. Bonar Law, Chancellor of the Exchequer, Mr. Balfour, Lord Curzon, and others to discuss the impending crisis. The immediate difficulty was the assumption, by the United States, of British obligations to J. P. Morgan and Company, amounting to $400,000,000. This item is always described in the correspondence of the two countries as the "Morgan overdraft." While this expression is accurate enough, it must be remembered that the English use of the banking word "overdraft" is somewhat different from the American, and does not carry the odious meaning attached to it in this country. The British had not "overdrawn" their account in the American sense of the term. The firm of J. P. Morgan had made advances to the British Government of not far from $400,000,000; that is, in reality the "overdraft" partook rather the nature of a loan. The time had arrived for settlement. The Balfour Commission to the United States had taken up this "overdraft" with Mr. McAdoo in June, 1917, and had left the country with the belief that it was to be paid out of the money obtained in the first Liberty Loan. Mr. McAdoo, however, insisted that no such promise had been made. The incident had led to a painful misunderstanding, and the meeting with Page and the Chancellor of the Exchequer was held in the hope of reaching a definite agreement. At the same time the whole financial plight of the Allies was discussed—a plight which Mr. Balfour himself described as the "brink of the precipice." It is a revelation also that on June 28, 1917, Great Britain had enough money in the United States to keep up exchange "for only one day more."

Telegram to the President

London, June 28, 1917.

SECRETARY OF STATE,

Washington.

Greatest Urgency.

Wholly confidential for the President and the Secretary of State and Secretary of the Treasury.

Mr. Balfour asked me to a conference at seven o'clock with him, the Chancellor of the Exchequer, and their financial advisers. It was disclosed that financial disaster to all the European Allies is imminent unless the United States Government advances to the British enough money to pay for British purchases in the United States as they fall due.

Bonar Law reports that only half enough has been advanced for June and that the British agents in the United States now have enough money to keep the exchange up for only one day more. If exchange with England fall exchange with all European allies also will immediately fall, and there will be a general collapse. Balfour understood that in addition to our other loans and our loans to France and Italy, we would advance to England enough to pay for all purchases by the British Government made in the United States. He authorizes me to say that they are now on the brink of a precipice, and unless immediate help be given financial collapse will follow. He is sending an explanatory telegram to Spring Rice.

I am convinced that these men are not overstating their case. Unless we come to their rescue we are all in danger of disaster. Great Britain will have to abandon the gold standard.

PAGE.

To the President

29 June, 1917, London.

DEAR MR. PRESIDENT:

The financial panic (it's hardly less) that this Government has raises the question, Why on earth do the British drift along till they reach a precipice? That's hard to answer. It's their way. They are too proud to acknowledge their predicament even to themselves until events force them to do so. Mr. Balfour informs me that the agreement that he reached in general terms with Mr. Mc-Adoo was this—that our Government would thenceforth lend (1) to France and Italy (and Russia?) the sums they would otherwise have to borrow from England (as they have all the while been borrowing) and (2) in addition lend to England whatever sums should be required to pay for British Government purchases in the United States. So much for that. I have no information whether that is Mr. McAdoo's understanding.

Now, Bonar Law assured me at the fearful financial conference to which they invited me that the Treasury Department had given Lever (the English financial agent) only half enough in June to meet the British Government's bills in the United States. Since they had reckoned on meeting all such bills from advances made by us, they find themselves unable to go further without our help. They have used all the gold they have in Canada. This, then, is the edge of the precipice. It came out that, a few weeks ago, the French came over here and persuaded the British that in addition to the French loan from the United States they were obliged to have the

British loans to them continued—for how long, I do not know. Bonar Law said, "We simply *had* to do it." The British, therefore, in spite of our help to France, still have France on their back and continue to give her money. I know that for a long time the British have felt that the French were not making a sufficient financial effort for themselves. "A Frenchman will lightly give his life for any cause that touches his imagination, but he will die rather than give a franc for any cause." There is a recurring fear here lest France in a moment of war-weariness may make a separate peace.

As things stand to-day, there is a danger of the fall of exchange and (perhaps) the abandonment of specie payments. These British run right into such a crisis before they are willing to confess their plight even to themselves.

They are not trying to lie down on us: they are too proud for that. Why they got into this predicament I do not fully know. I know nothing of what arrangements were made with them except what Mr. Balfour tells me. It seems to me that some definite understanding ought to have been reduced to writing. But here they are in this predicament, which I duly reported by telegram.

It is unlucky that "crises" come in groups—two or three at once. But the submarine situation is as serious as the financial. I have a better knowledge of that than I have of the financial situation. But in one respect they are alike—the British drive ahead, concealing their losses, their misfortunes, and their mistakes till they are on the very brink of disaster: that is their temperament. Into this submarine peril (the Germans are fast winning in this crucial activity—there's no doubt about that) I have gone pretty thoroughly with their naval men and their shipping authorities. Admiral Sims has reached the same conclusions that I have reached—independently, from his point of view. The immediate grave danger for the present lies here. If the present rate of destruction of shipping goes on, the war will end before a victory is won. And time is of the essence of the problem; and the place where it will be won is in the waters of the approach to this Kingdom —not anywhere else. The full available destroyer power that can by any method be made available must be concentrated in this area within weeks (not months). There are not in the two navies half destroyers enough: improvised destroyers must be got. There must be enough to provide convoys for every ship that is worth saving. Merely arming them affords the minimum of protection. Armed merchantmen are destroyed every day. Convoyed ships escape—almost all. That is the convincing actual experience.

If we had not come into the war when we did, and if we had not begun action and given help with almost miraculous speed, I do not say that the British would have been actually beaten (tho' this may have followed), but I do say that they would have quickly been on a paper money basis, thereby bringing down the financial situation of all the European Allies; and the submarine success of the Germans would or might have caused a premature peace. They were in worse straits than they ever confessed to themselves. And now we are all in bad straits because of this submarine destruction of shipping. One sea-going tug now may be worth more than a dozen ships next year.

Yours very faithfully,
WALTER H. PAGE.

Mr. McAdoo, in his discussion of the financial situation, differed somewhat with British representatives in Washington. He declared that neither he nor any other responsible American official had promised to pay the "Morgan overdraft" out of the proceeds of the first Liberty Loan, and insisted that before making such engagements the American Government must have rather more information about British finances and British purchases in the United States. He also expressed himself as rather confused by the number of Englishmen in the United States who professed to represent the British Government and was especially puzzled by Lord Northcliffe's presence. "We have every desire," he wrote, "to be friendly and obliging. We have given conclusive evidence of this, but in order to avoid future misunderstanding it would be wise to have it understood that nothing shall be considered as agreed to until signed memoranda or documents have been exchanged." What especially hurt the feelings of the British, however, was Mr. McAdoo's remark that "America's coöperation cannot mean that America can assume the entire cost of financing the war." This statement, and the difficulties arising from the general situation, led Mr. Bonar Law to frame a memorandum for Page, which succinctly describes Great Britain's financial efforts since August, 1914, and sets forth with the utmost frankness the conditions that prevailed when the United States came to the rescue. It is therefore a document of great historic importance, and was immediately sent by Page to Washington.

The Chancellor of the Exchequer to Page

The Chancellor of the Exchequer has seen Mr. Page July 14th and would be much obliged if Mr. Secretary Balfour would cause the following note in reply to be communicated to Mr. Page. The Chancellor of the Exchequer of course accepts Mr. McAdoo's statement that "At no time, directly or indirectly, has the Secretary of the Treasury or any one connected with his Department promised to pay the Morgan overdraft." In any event, this question of past misunderstandings is of small consequence as compared with the question as to whether the financial interests of the alliance make this repayment necessary or advisable at the present time. But in view of what passed at the Chancellor of the Exchequer's interview with Mr. Page, the Chancellor of the Exchequer thinks it right to quote the actual words received by cable from Sir C. Spring Rice on April 9th which were the foundation of what he said on that occasion. Spring Rice telegraphed: "Sir R. Crawford desires the following to be communicated to the Chancellor of the Exchequer. I told the Secretary of the Treasury last night that you appreciated and concurred in his proposals. He was very gratified and asked me to convey his compliments. I mentioned to him the four considerations referred to in paragraph two of your telegram. He agreed that repayment of overdraft on four hundred million dollars would be a first call on the loan. . . . This morning Governor Harding called, at the request of the Secretary, and confirmed the views expressed by the latter on the above points. This evening I went over the matter again with the Counsellor of the State Department, who fully concurred that our overdraft should be a first charge." There are several indications in Mr. McAdoo's note that he desires above all a fuller and freer communication of facts on our part. We have never desired or intended to keep any reserves from him as to our financial position. On the other hand, it has been our preoccupation to bring home to him exactly what that position is. Any specific question we will answer. In the meantime the following figures are presented in the belief that they are the figures most relevant to present issues:

(A) Mr. McAdoo points out: "That America's coöperation cannot mean that America can assume the entire burden of financing the war." How much less than this has been expressly asked of it is exemplified in the following table of assistance rendered to the European Allies by the United States and the United Kingdom respectively since the date of the entry of America into the war.

Financial assistance from April first to July fourteenth, nineteen hundred and seventeen:

Advanced by United Kingdom to France £56,037,000 sterling; to Russia, £78,472,000; to Italy, £47,760,000; to Belgium, including Congo, £8,035,000; to minor Allies, £3,545,000. Total, £193,849,000 sterling.

Advanced by United States [to France] $310,000,000; [to Russia] nil; [to Italy] $100,000,000; [to Belgium] $15,000,000; [to minor Allies] $2,000,000; total, $427,000,000, equals pounds sterling, ninety million.

The advances by the United States equal, roughly, £90,000,000 against the advances by the United Kingdom of nearly £194,000,000. Russia has been promised $100,000,000 but it is understood that she has not yet received any cash installments. For Belgian relief total amounts promised $45,000,000; Serbia total amount promised $3,000,000.

The Chancellor of the Exchequer gratefully acknowledges that the United States Treasury have advanced $686,000,000 to this country in addition to the above sums to the other Allies.

But he invites Mr. McAdoo's particular attention to the fact that even since America came into the war the financial assistance afforded to the other Allies by the United Kingdom has been more than double the assistance afforded them by the United States, and that the assistance the United

Kingdom has afforded these other Allies much exceeds the assistance she has herself received from the United States.

(B) The United States Treasury have so far limited their assistance to expenditure incurred by the Allies within the United States, rightly recognizing that such assistance involves a much less onerous burden than a financial assistance abroad. The United Kingdom have been unable to adopt this attitude toward their Allies but have supported the burden of their expenditure in all parts of the world. Without this support the Allies would have been unable to obtain the supplies of food and munitions which have been essential to their prosecution of the war.

To such an extent has the above been the case that up to the present time, the United Kingdom is still financing the expenditure of Russia in the United States.

(C) The total expenditure out of the British Exchequer between April first, nineteen hundred and seventeen, and July fourteenth, nineteen hundred and seventeen, amounted to £825,109,000 sterling, of which pounds sterling £131,245,000 was met from loans raised in the United States. Both these figures relate to expenditure and income brought to account out of date fourteenth.

(D) The financial burden upon the Exchequer of the United Kingdom did not begin, however, on April first last. The total expenditure between April first, 1914, and March 31st, 1917, amounted to £4,362,798,000 sterling which added to the expenditure of £825,109,000 sterling since April first, 1917, makes a total expenditure of £5,161,471,000 sterling. It is after having supported an expenditure of this magnitude for three years that the United Kingdom venture to appeal to the United States of America for sympathetic consideration in financial discussion where the excessive urgency of her need and the precariousness of her position may somewhat impart a tone of insistence to her requests for assistance which would be out of place in ordinary circumstances.

A statement is appended at the end of this note for Mr. McAdoo's information showing precisely how this sum of five billion pounds has been financed up to date. The proceeds of the overdraft in New York are included under the heading of the ways and means advances. This statement included several particulars which have not been communicated to Parliament and is to be regarded, like all the other figures cited in this note, as being only for the confidential information of the United States Government.

(E) The following statement shows the expenditure and receipts of the British Government in New York from the first April to the fourteenth July nineteen hundred and seventeen.

Payments out of the treasury account in New York for the purchase of commodities and interest due, $602,000,000.

Purchase of exchange (e. g., the cost of all wheat purchases for Allies) is included in this figure *inter alia* during the greater part of the period in question) $529,000,000, total $1,131,000,000.

Loans from United States Government, $685,000,000.

British treasury notes (sundry munitions contracts), $27,000,000.

Repayments by French and Italian governments, $134,000,000.

Gold, $246,000,000.

Sale of securities, $58,000,000; miscellaneous, $19,000,000; total, $1,169,000,000.

(F) It will be seen from the preceding statement that gold and securities were realized during the period in question (for the most part during June) to the extent of $304,000,000. The impossibility of the United Kingdom's continuing to supplement American government assistance on this scale is shown by the following facts.

Gold.   We have exported to the United States since the commencement of the war (including gold lately earmarked for the New York Federal Reserve Bank) a sum of $305,000,000 in actual gold.   This has all been sent on behalf of the United Kingdom, but a considerable part has been borrowed or purchased from the other Allies. In addition a fairly substantial amount has been despatched to other destinations.   This represents an enormous effort of which the reserves of the United States have obtained the benefit.

The United Kingdom now have left about £50,000,000 in the Bank of England's reserve, £28,500,000 in the currency note reserve, and an unknown amount estimated at a maximum of £50,000,000 with the joint stock banks In addition there is a sum of about £10,000,000 at the disposal of the Treasury but not included in any published reserve.   This makes a total of about £140,000,000 There are virtually no government bonds in circulation This is about six per cent. of our banking liabilities and considerably less than allotted circulation of the government bonds in the United States.

The amount of this government loan which we could part with, without destroying the confidence upon which our credit rests, is inconsiderable.

Securities.   Before the Treasury initiated their official mobilization of dollar securities large amounts were disposed of through private channels and also by the Bank of England, who were systematically engaged in the disposal of Dutch government securities in New York.

The following figures relate only to the treasury scheme value of securities purchased, $770,000,000; value of securities obtained on deposit as a loan, $1,130,000,000

Total, $1,900,000,000. The above has been disposed of as follows: Sold in New York, $750,000,000; deposited as security against loans, $600,000,000; deposited as security against call loan, $400,000,000; still in hand, $150,000,000; total, $1,900,000,000 (all figures approximate). We have now obtained virtually all the dollar securities available in this country and, in view of penalties now attached, it is believed that the amount of saleable securities still in private hands is now of very small dimensions. The balance in hand can only be disposed of gradually and is not in any case an important amount.

In short, our resources available for payments in America are exhausted. Unless the United States Government can meet in full our expenses in America, including exchange, the whole financial fabric of the alliance will collapse. This conclusion will be a matter not of months but of days.

The question is one of which it is necessary to take a large view. If matters continue on the same basis as during the last few weeks a financial disaster of the first magnitude cannot be avoided. In the course of August the enemy will receive the encouragement of which he stands in so great need, at the moment of the war when perhaps he needs it most.

Mr. McAdoo suggests that the settlement of joint allied purchasing arrangements must precede any promises from him of financial support in August. His Majesty's Government do not know how to interpret this statement. They are doing what they can to promote the establishment of such arrangements and at the end of June prepared a detailed scheme, on lines which they had been given to understand would commend themselves to the United States Government, for submission to the other Allies, but the settlement depends upon the progress of events in America and the acquiescence of the other Allies concerned. They will instruct Sir C. Spring Rice to communicate unofficially the details to the United States Government immediately without waiting for replies from the other Allies. His Majesty's Government cannot believe that, if these or other natural and unavoidable causes of delay are operative for reasons which may be out of their control, financial support will be withheld and a catastrophe precipitated.

As regards Mr. McAdoo's concluding passage, the Chancellor of the Exchequer desires to say that Lord Northcliffe is the duly authorized representative of His Majesty's Government to conduct all financial negotiations on their behalf. Lord Northcliffe has, however, suggested that the United States Government would themselves prefer that someone with political experience such as an ex-cabinet member should be asked to cross to the United States for the purpose of dealing with the financial situation. If this is the desire of the United States Government, His Majesty's Government would gladly comply with it.

To the Secretary of State

London, August 2, 1917.

SECRETARY OF STATE,
     Washington.
          August 2, 3 P. M.   Confidential for the Secretary and
          President only.
     Mr. Balfour has gone over with me the telegram he sent July thirty to Spring Rice for McAdoo about exchange. He represents the position as most perilous. He hopes that the President has seen it and will cause a reply to be sent at earliest possible time.

PAGE.

These documents make clear the financial disaster from which the United States saved the Allies, for, in a brief time, all difficulties and misunderstandings were adjusted, and American advances, to the extent of nearly $12,000,000,000, went with clock-like regularity to support the great cause.

CHAPTER XV

THE LAST LETTERS

OF ALL the utterances of President Wilson, probably the answer to Pope Benedict XV, in August, 1917, gave Page the greatest satisfaction. His Holiness had appealed to the warring powers to cease their battles, to restore the political conditions of Europe as they had existed before 1914, and to settle outstanding problems on the basis of arbitration, general condonation, and Christian charity. President Wilson, paying due respect to the source from which the proposal came, rejected it in words that sped like lightning through two hemispheres and put a new spirit into the efforts of the Allies. "The object of the war," said the President, "is to deliver the free peoples of the world from the menace and the actual power of a vast military establishment, controlled by an irresponsible government, which, having secretly planned to dominate the world, proceeded to carry the plan out without regard either to the sacred obligations of treaty or the long-established practices and long-cherished principles of international action and honour, which chose its own time for the war, delivered its blow fiercely and suddenly, stopped at no barrier, either of law or of mercy; swept a whole continent within the tide of blood—not the blood of soldiers only, but the blood of innocent women and of children also, and of the helpless poor; and now stands, balked but not defeated, the enemy of four fifths of the world." It was an eloquent description of the origin of the war and the spirit with which Germany had waged hostilities and one can imagine Page's pleasure in reading it. Nor would it have been more than human nature had he felt a personal gratification. For the President's interpretation was precisely the one that Page had been setting forth for three years. From the day the Germans invaded Belgium, the Ambassador, in letter after letter, had described the object of the war, as the deliverance "of the free peoples of the world from the menace and the actual power of a vast military establishment, controlled by an irresponsible government." The necessary conclusion, in the President's reply—that the United States, in making peace, should have no negotiations with the Hohenzollern government, but would insist on dealing only with the responsible representatives of the German people—was a plan which Page would naturally approve.

"As I promptly telegraphed you," Page wrote in reference to this message, "and as, of course, you have heard through many channels, your reply to the Pope received a most enthusiastic welcome here, not only because it meets with universal approval: there's a deeper reason than that. It expresses definitely the moral and the deep and clear political reason for the war—the freeing of the world, including the German people, from the German military autocracy; and it expresses this better and with more force than it has ever been expressed by anybody on this side the world. You have made acceptable peace-terms clearer, not only to the enemy, but also to the Allies, than they have ever before been made known. All these nations here have so many relatively unimportant and so many purely selfish aims that their minds run on. Here you come setting forth the one big thing worth fighting for—the one big moral and political aim—no revenge, no mere boundary rectifications, no subsidiary thing to confuse the main purpose. This gives moral leadership to the whole war; and the British know and feel this."

To the President

London, Sept. 25, 1917.

DEAR MR. PRESIDENT:

There has, I think, been no other stroke so effective—apart from our coming into the war—as your firm announcement in your letter to the Pope that we cannot deal with the present government of Germany unless satisfactory guarantees are given directly by the German people. This had been said here but never, I think, said with official sanction and surely never with convincing force. Now that *you* have said it, it takes precedence over every other formula of necessary demands. It is, of course, *the* necessary demand, the necessary condition of peace. It has had a tremendous effect upon British opinion and British resolution.

And so far as I can judge, its effect in Germany has been and continues to be supreme. The violence with which it is resented and the mobilization of official opinion against it tell the story. It is worth more than the winning of a dozen great battles.

Of course, it means far more coming from you than it could be made to mean coming from any subject of a "crowned" republic. The "crowned" is the trouble. Then, too, the British do not trust even the German people. Neither do I, for that matter. But this is not directly to the point. For no popular government—even of a nation wholly depraved and villainous, if there were such a nation—could ever get the power or develop the will to play the German Government's rôle. I can't judge what chance there is of a revolution in Germany, but, if there be a chance, your declaration strengthens it and if

there have hitherto been no chance, your declaration
suggests it. Besides, it has planted firmly in the minds
of all the Allies the real aim of the war. Everything else
is secondary to this aim.

Of course, your declaration is only part and parcel of the
commanding influence of all that you say; and whatever
you say goes further home both in Germany and among
the Allies than all things that all other men say.

The British are full not only of gratitude but of admiration of the way we go about the task; and their
curiosity to know all that we are doing is pathetic. I have
just come, for instance, from lunch with Mr. Asquith
and Mr. Winston Churchill, who talked and asked about
nothing but our preparations. They have both been in
France very lately and they are full of praise of what they
saw and heard of our Expeditionary Force. They freely
acknowledge that an undesirable peace would have been
forced on the Allies by this time if we had not come in.
So, too, did M. Schneider, the French Krupp, who was at
this luncheon. The same frank confession comes out
everywhere now. It was freely spoken, for instance, the
other day when Balfour, Geddes, and Jellicoe, and I talked
for two hours.

I wish it were possible for some proper person to come
here—a good public speaker—who could explain in some
detail and somewhat officially just what we are doing and
how we are doing it in the United States. The curiosity
of the British Government and public is insatiable and
their admiration unbounded.

I have heard nothing more about the reported naval
misunderstanding[1] than I telegraphed a few days ago

---

[1] The reference is to a report which had reached Washington, that the British
naval authorities were not dealing fairly with the American Navy and were concealing information.

after my long conference with Balfour, Geddes, and Jellicoe. They are much disturbed and they evidently think that some mischiefmaker is at work. They protest that they have been perfectly frank and have opened all doors of information to us and given the profoundest consideration to every suggestion and request that has come from us, and that still they hear of dissatisfaction at Washington. I suspect that they have a fear lest Pollen,[1] a British writer and lecturer on naval subjects, now in the United States, has been stirring up trouble. It seems that the Admiralty and the Navy here have never been able to please Pollen or to win his approval. Whether my guess about Pollen be correct or not, something is wrong in fact or in gossip. They are very eager for Admiral Benson himself to come here. I asked Jellicoe why he didn't go to Washington, and his reply was: "The problem itself is here. I wish the head of your naval staff himself to see that we withhold nothing. If *he* understand it, no trouble can come from subordinates."

Geddes, by the way, the new First Lord of the Admiralty, is making a very favourable impression on the Government and on public opinion; and I think deservedly and properly. He is an extraordinarily forcible man. He ran away when a boy and worked in a saw-mill camp in West Virginia. Subsequently he had a valuable and (I think) quite extensive experience in railroad work in the United States and learned American railroad management. The result was that he worked his way, when he came back here, into the chief manager's place of one of the big English railways, and made a great reputation as a manager of men—as a man of great force who brings things to pass. A year or so ago he was put in charge of

---

[1]Mr. Arthur H. Pollen, a severe critic of the Admiralty.

the big transportation problem of the British in France—against the wishes of the army commanders. He went there with their prejudice against him, but he completely won their approval and their warm praise by the way he did the job. They made him a Brigadier-General. When Lloyd George concluded that he wanted the utmost push in the Admiralty, he made Geddes First Lord. This required that he should be a member of Parliament. The member for Cambridge resigned to make room for him and Geddes was elected in his place. Then they made him an Admiral. Some wag remarked that next week they'd probably make Geddes Archbishop! It was a new experience to take a civilian railroad manager—a man who has no politics that anybody ever heard of and who has had no political experience and who didn't even know many of the political figures or managers—and give him one of the very foremost Cabinet positions. When he took office those who did not feel some prejudice against him at least looked at him with a question mark. Already he has won the confidence and enthusiasm of his associates, as he did of the army officers in France.

I have seen a good deal of him, and there is no doubt of his clear head, his sound judgment, and his most uncommon energy and directness. One nickname they have for him is "The Yank." If I had to bet, I'd bet on him. I don't for a moment believe that this fellow will play any tricks on us or on anybody else. I should say that he now has only one aim in life and that is to win the war and to make the Navy do its utmost to win it.

Every ship now brings special men sent by many departments of our Government to get information—army men, naval men, aircraft men, Red Cross men; and after I have put them into the proper channels, I try to follow every one of them and to ask if they've got all they came for. They all report the most courteous treatment and success in their quests. Several departments of the British Government have volunteered the request that I have them promptly informed if any accredited Americans fail to receive what they ask for.

We are fast accumulating war trophies from the air raids on London. Pieces of shells—from the British anti-aircraft guns—fell on my roof last night during the half-hour battle. We were at dinner and we concluded that it was as well to be hit with full stomachs as with empty ones. So we finished the meal about the time the battle ended. During these moonlit evenings we receive an attack every night—always, of course, with loss of life greater than the newspapers are allowed to report. Two bombs fell last night within a few hundred yards of Buckingham Palace and two more still nearer the Houses of Parliament. But it is hard to believe that the German airmen knew just what buildings they came near hitting. The guns at least keep them at a great height. A fortnight ago a bomb wrecked a street so near my house that two or three seconds difference would have caused it to fall on the square where I live—two or three seconds difference in the time of its release from the aëroplane. We are, therefore, now literally in the war. We pay singularly little attention to it—one gets used to it—and there are, after all, singularly few casualties—about twenty people killed and seventy-five hurt every time. We expect a raid and a battle every night while the moon lasts.

But this is an incident of the war unworthy of mention.

Believe me, Mr. President,
Yours faithfully,
WALTER H. PAGE.

The few remaining letters, written at long intervals, require no comment.

To the President

London, 22 December, 1917.

DEAR MR. PRESIDENT:

. . . The Lansdowne[1] letter was used as an occasion to demand a clearer and simpler explanation of the aims of the war. I do not quite see how such a demand—which itself is one evidence of a weary depression—can be satisfied by thumb-nail catch phrases. Mr. Balfour, as I dare say you have read, declared in the House of Commons two nights ago that your recent speeches and letters were as able as any state papers produced in the whole history of the world. Everybody points to them as the preëminent formulation of war aims, and yet the cry continues here for some summary that the man in the street and the man in the trenches can understand. All this will pass with the New Year mood.

But there is one thing that I wish the British would themselves say more plainly and concretely—that the only way to security is to overthrow the German military autocracy, so as to show that this implies at least the unhorsing of the Emperor. I should not say positively that the dynastic principle prevents. But it has something to do with preventing a clear cry. Almost everywhere in Europe—everywhere outside of France and Switzerland—men seem yet unable to think of government without kings. Something of the old divinity doth yet hedge them. Even in England there is a hesitancy to speak out plainly about crowned villains. The Tsar

---

[1] A letter written by Lord Lansdowne, on November 29, 1917, and published in the *Daily Telegraph*. It contended that the war had lasted too long, and was generally criticized as favouring an unsatisfactory peace.

himself found much sympathy here in certain circles. The vague fear lest royalty here may come upon an evil day shows itself by irrelevant and unnecessary outbursts in praise of the King; and the argument is overworked that a throne is necessary to hold the Empire together. . . . . .

> With all good wishes,
> Yours faithfully,
> WALTER H. PAGE.

To the President

London, January 16, 1918.

DEAR MR. PRESIDENT:

You know Lord Reading[1] and have taken measure of him, but the following facts and gossip may interest you: He is one of the ablest Englishmen living—everybody concedes that. See and compare the view taken of Disraeli, the other Hebrew Earl, by his political enemies. As between the two my judgment would be in favour of Reading. He is not so spectacular as old Dizzy was, but he is far sounder. I doubt if Dizzy was honest, and Reading is. He is one of the most brilliant and able members of the Bar. He has himself told me that he worked for years from early hours to early hours again day in and day out—a prodigy of industry. He became skilful, especially in financial cases, and his fees were prodigious.

Lord Reading does not give up the Lord Chief Justiceship. He remarked to me the other day that his Ambassadorship would be temporary. Lady Reading told Mrs. Page that they expected to be gone only three months. But I take it that he will not return till the end of the war.

I have reason to believe (although I do not know) that

---

[1]Lord Reading had recently been appointed British Ambassador to the United States.

an effort was made to induce Mr. Balfour and then Lord Grey to go as Ambassador to Washington. I know that the appointment was offered to Northcliffe. He didn't care to be away from London so long lest he should lose his grip on the general management of things, which in his inmost soul he thinks he holds and which, to a degree, he does hold. The belief, moreover, is widespread that he may become Prime Minister if Lloyd George should not last till peace come. I think there is no doubt that to do a concrete job Lord Reading will succeed, during war time, better than any man who was considered for the post. But if when the war is over Lord Grey should go, we should have the best possible representative of English tradition and English character. Yet I think he never will, although he is going after the war to deliver lectures at Yale and elsewhere.

Of course, the immediate problems to be met in the relations of the two Governments will continue to be financial—till we have to slacken our pace. The British, God knows, need money, but God knows also that they are not slow in making their wants known. I doubt if anybody, but the Germans, will ever wage war on less than twice what it ought to cost. But, if it could be more extravagantly conducted than they (the British) conduct it, I can't imagine how it could be done.

There is going on a visit to the United States on the invitation of some of our ecclesiastical organizations the Most Reverend and Rt. Honourable His Grace the Lord Archbishop of York whose name (which is never used) is Cosmo Gordon Lang, D.D., LL.D., D.C.L., D.Litt. &c., &c., &c.— and he signs his name Cosmo Ebor. He comes of Scotch-Irish stock. He is the best representative of the best English clerical life—a simple, humble, learned, right-minded man of charm and fine manners and fine feeling.

He is most eager to meet you and you will enjoy him. Of course his proper approach (he's a Peer Spiritual) is through his Ambassador. To mortals of humble rank, such as President Eliot, I have given him letters. The Archbishop at one end of the line and Reading at the other—they make good representatives of Notable England.

There is a very general uneasiness here about the expected offensive by the Germans in France, for the feeling is that they are willing to sacrifice their whole army for Paris or Calais and that they are going to make their most desperate effort regardless of the cost in men or in anything else. How true this is everybody can guess for himself. But it seems probable, to say the least. Their chance is better than it will be after we get a great trained army in France. There is a sense, too, in which such a decisive effort will be welcomed here. Nothing is printed and little is said in public about the constant danger of labour troubles in this Kingdom, but such a danger has always to be taken into account. The Briton, nobleman or labourer, is not going to give out or give up, but it costs him more and more in money and in anxiety to keep his whole force in the field, in the factory, in the mine, and on the land, going at full strength, than it would cost but for this constant labour burden.

"After the War" hasn't come yet. But I recall a remark that Edward Grey made to me before the war, that Labour would in a decade control many governments. A frequent prediction now made here by well-informed Englishmen is that it will control the government of Great Britain. The Labour Party is already playing for supremacy.

It's a quieter, sadder, more serious time and mood than we have before had in England. Everybody feels that we are approaching great and perhaps decisive events; and they all thank God for the United States and its President.

Yours very heartily,

WALTER H. Page.

There certainly could be no more appropriate conclusion to this series than the following letter, which probably sets forth as eloquently as it has ever been set forth the spirit that made inevitable Allied victory:

To the President

London, March 7, 1918.

DEAR MR. PRESIDENT:

The complete break-down of Russia and the present German occupation of so much of that Empire as she wants, together with the surrender of Rumania, have had a very strong effect on both sections of public opinion here as I interpret the British mind. In the enormously dominant section these untoward events have stiffened the war resolution. They say that Germany must now be whipped to a finish. Else she will have doubled her territory, got raw materials and food, probably opened a way to Asia, strengthened the Turks, and will hold the peoples of her new territory as vassals—to exploit them and their lands in preparation for another war for further conquests. The war lord will be more firmly seated than before. Only if her armies be literally whipped will the German military caste be thrown out of power. This probably means a very long war yet.

The minority section of opinion—so far as I can judge, it is a small minority—has the feeling that such a decisive military victory cannot be won; that the enemies of Germany, allowing her to keep her Eastern gains, must soon make the best bargain they can in the West. Of course this plan would leave the German military caste in power and would be a defeat for the Allies in so far as a fair chance for a permanent peace is concerned. It would leave at least European Russia to German mercy, and the Baltic and Black seas practically in German control.

Lord Lansdowne and his friends (how numerous they are nobody knows) are the loudest spokesmen for such a peace as might be made now, especially if Belgium can be restored and an agreement reached about Alsace-Lorraine. But it is talked much of in Asquith circles that the time may come when this policy (its baldness somewhat modified) may be led by Mr. Asquith. He has up to this time patriotically supported the Government. But he is very generally suspected of intrigue, and his friends openly predict that at what they regard as a favourable moment he will take his cue. I myself can hardly believe this. I do not believe that even a party political victory lies in that direction. But a virtual surrender to the Germans would, if this peace-plan should be successful.

The dominant section is sorely grieved about the present state of Russia. But they refuse to be discouraged by it. They recall how Napoleon overran the most of Europe and how the French held none of his conquests after his fall.

The danger that the present government is in here, comes, it seems to me, not mainly from the split in public opinion that I have described, but from the personal enemies of Mr. Lloyd George and his Government. They make the most of the dismissal of Jellicoe and of Robertson and of the appointment of Beaverbrook and Northcliffe and of the closeness of the Government to agitating newspapers—whether the newspapers run the Government or the Government runs the newspapers doesn't matter: they are, their enemies say, too closely intertwined.

It is certain that Lloyd George keeps power mainly if not solely because he is the most energetic man in sight. Many who support him do not like him personally. But nobody doubts his supreme earnestness to win the war, and everybody holds that this is the only task now worth while. This feeling has saved him in both recent political "crises." After the last one, he remarked to me with an exultant manner: "They don't seem to want anybody else —yet, do they?" His dismissal of Robertson has been accepted in the interest of greater unity of military control, but that was a dangerous rapids he shot; for he didn't handle the boat very tactfully. The previous dismissal of Jellicoe has now just come up, rather bitterly, in the House of Commons. Whether these two incidents are quiescent, it is hard to tell. From the inside I hear that both were necessary because of the inability both of the great sailor and of the great soldier to work in administrative harness with other people. It may very well be true that the place for both is in fight, not in administration. Such surely was the case with Kitchener.

Yet there is a certain danger to the Government also because some of them are thought to be wearing out. Parliament itself—I mean the House of Commons—is thought to be going stale: it has had an enormously long life. The Prime Minister, though a tough and robust man, has increasingly frequent little breakdowns. Bonar Law seems and is very weary. Mr. Balfour's health is not uniformly robust, and his enemies call him old and languid. But, just when this criticism finds a voice, he makes a clearer statement than anybody else has made and the threatened storm passes. Still, the Government, like all other governments in Europe now, is overworked and tired.

But I believe British opinion to be sound, and British

endurance is only having its first real test. The people here are forever accusing one another, especially those in authority, of weakness. They have always done so. It is a sort of national vice, which it is well to remember in all outbursts of dissatisfaction. I form my opinion from what I know and see of two opposite and widely separated sections of society. Labour—there has been grave trouble with Labour since the beginning of the war—in its recent manifesto stood quite firm and resolute. The "lower classes" are undoubtedly in favour of a fight to a finish. The Tommy is made of as good fighting material as there is in the world. He knows enough to be bulldoggish and not enough to have any philosophic doubts. I was much impressed a little while ago with the reasons that Lord Derby gave me for regarding the present British Army as the best that the world has ever seen. I reminded him, when he had enumerated his reasons, that all that he had said suggested to me that for those very reasons there would soon be a better army. He was gracious enough not to dispute my contention.

The aristocracy—the real aristocracy—too are plucky to the last degree. That's one virtue that they have supremely. They do not wince. They seem actually to remember the hard plight that Napoleon put them in. They licked him. Hence, they can lick anybody. The separation of this island from the Continent and the ancient mixture here of the breeds of men produced a kind of man that stands up in a fight—no doubt about that —whether he be a bejewelled and arrogant aristocrat and reactionary or a forgotten and neglected Hodge of the soil.

I was at a dinner of old Peers at the Athenæum Club— a group of old cocks that I meet once in a while and have come to know pretty well and ever to marvel at. I think

every one is past seventy—several of them past eighty.
On this occasion I was the only commoner present.   The
talk went on about every imaginable thing—reminis-
cences of Browning, the years of good vintages of port,
the excellence of some court opinions handed down in the
United States by quite obscure judges—why shouldn't
they be got out of the masses of law reports and published as classics?—wouldn't it have been well if the
King had gone and spent his whole time at the front and
on the fleet,—what's an English King for anyhow?—then
a defense of Reading; and why should the Attorney
General or the Lord Chief Justice be allowed out of the
Kingdom at all at such a time?

"Call in the chief steward. . . . Here, steward,
what's that noise?"

"A hair raid, milord."

"How long has it been going on?"

"Forty minutes, milord."

"I must be deaf," said the old fellow, with an inquiring
look at the company.   Everybody else had heard it, but
we've learned to take these things for granted and nobody
had interrupted the conversation to speak of it.   Then
the old man spoke up again.

"Well, there's nothing we can do to protect His Excellency.   Damn the air raid.   Pass the port."

Then the talk went on about the ignorance and the
commonness of modern British governments—most modern governments, in fact.   French statesmen—most of
'em common fellows, and Italians and Germans—ach!
What swine!   "Think of that fellow Von Kühlmann.[1]   I
lent him a valuable book and the rogue never returned it.
Did you know Kühlmann?"

---

[1] An important member of the German Embassy in London under Prince
Lichnowsky.

"But," turning to me, "you are to be congratulated. You have a *gentleman* for your President. How do you do it? That breed seems to be out of a job in most countries."

Not one of those old fellows drove to the club. They can't get gasoline and they have no horses. Nor can cabs be got after ten o'clock. When the firing and bomb dropping had ceased, the question arose whether it was safe to walk home. My car had come and I took five of them in it—one on the front with the driver. As each got out at his door he bade me an almost affectionate goodnight. One of them said, "By our combined forces the God of our Fathers—not the barbarous Prussian Gott—will see us through."

There's no sham about these old masters of empire. They feel a proprietary interest in the King, in the Kingdom, in everything British. Every man of them had done some distinguished service and so have the sons of most of them; and at least half of them have lost grandsons or sons in the war, to which they never allude. An enemy might kill them if he could get to them, but change them or scare them or make them surrender—never. Take 'em all in all, for downright human interest, I don't know where you'd find their equals. Take them as mere phenomena of human society and of a social system—well, that's another story. But they, and their like, are not going to give up in this war.

Well, a little before that, I met once a week for three or four weeks at dinner about a dozen Labour leaders, who good-humouredly wrangled with one another and with me, they being of a disputatious turn. It's a pretty good world to them, on the whole; but economic society is organized with gross injustice and their misfortune is that they must set it right. On many things they can't agree with one another; but on one thing they are of like mind: the employer wasn't fair before the war and he isn't fair now. The war brings no reason to their minds why they should surrender. Let *him* surrender, rather. *But* they wouldn't desert the country. They'll beat the hog of an employer, but they'll keep up the war, and a larger measure of democracy will follow. Most of these men are keen-minded, able, pugnacious and, like all breeds of the John Bull stock, *tenacious*. They have a case—I'm disposed to think, a good case—which they urge most often by bad methods. They *will* have a larger measure of democracy. The first concrete form that it has taken is the new Franchise Act which doubles the number of voters. There is now an approximation to one vote for every man over twenty-one and for every woman over thirty. Other such concrete changes will come—perhaps a Labour government, certainly a Labour government if all Labour holds together. One of these fellows goes on a crutch from a war wound. They are not for a peace that will soon end in another war.

As I make it out, it is chiefly in political and philosophic circles that hopelessness finds a home. Lord Lansdowne belongs to both these groups, to one by temperament, the other by training. I ran across him a fortnight ago. He had, for an old man who is far from well, an almost unseemly gaiety of spirit, and he insisted on talking almost wholly about agriculture. I had sent to our Agricultural Department for certain of its publications, which greatly interested him. I almost forgive him his vagueness, cut bias of political thought because of his sound agricultural knowledge.

I set out to write you, Mr. President, more about our own affairs here rather than this weary stuff about the curious and admirable and stolid and eternally baffling carnivorous and amphibious animal that inhabits this island. But I'll tire you with a longer letter. Our own affairs here are, I think, going well—in most respects surely. The Embassy is war-weary in this sense—that the staff has one sick man—one after another—all the while. The London winter all indoors and the failure of some of the best workers to take exercise—that's the trouble; but it's not serious. A week on the South Shore sets the digestion going again.

I am trying to get together some information in an authoritative way which I hope will be useful to House in his preparation for the Peace Conference. It is an interesting task as well as baffling. And much of my time is taken in making sure that our several groups of people, such as the Shipping Board group, the War Trade Board group, etc., are getting on well with the several departments of the Government, as, up to this time, they have. The British try to play the game openly and gratefully.

My fears for our future dealings centre about trade jealousies.

Yours faithfully,
WALTER H. PAGE.

EPILOGUE

PAGE died at Pinehurst, North Carolina, December 21, 1918; the first two volumes of "The Life and Letters of Walter H. Page" were published in October, 1922. In both the United States and Great Britain the disclosure of the great part he had played in the war and the literary charm and permanent historical value of his letters, made a deep impression. Americans recognized that in supporting the Allied cause from the beginning of the war, in constantly placing before President Wilson the great facts in the conflict, in insisting that the power of the United States should inevitably be used to bring about the defeat of the Central Empires, Page was preaching Americanism of the loftiest kind. Especially impressive was the recognition that the Ambassadorship and the policies and opinions it made vital merely formed the climax of a consistent career. With Page's past in his own country—with his interest in the democratic progress of the common man—any other attitude than that of allegiance to the Allied cause would have been unthinkable. Since his death several memorials, in this country and in England, have paid tribute to Page's services in several fields. The little town in which the future Ambassador was born, Cary, North Carolina, has named its institution for secondary education "The Walter H. Page High School"—an appropriate testimony to his struggles for popular instruction in the South. His college, Randolph-Macon, in Virginia, dedicated, in December, 1923, the "Walter Hines Page Library." North Carolina, the state which Page loved so well, but which at times had so misunderstood him—the old boyhood home to which his heart longingly turned in those last days in England, and to which, broken by his five years' Ambassadorship, he came back to die—has placed his portrait in the State Capitol at Raleigh—a replica of the painting, by Philip Laszlo, that hangs in the American Embassy in London.

A great school of international relations has been founded at Johns Hopkins University—the institution at which Page, from 1876 to 1878, was one of the first twenty Fellows. It had been Page's plan, on his return to the United States, to devote his life to improving relations between peoples—not only between the United States and Great Britain, but the United States and the whole world. "My fears for our future dealings," he writes in the last letter of the present book, "centre about trade jealousies." The sentence contains much to set his countrymen thinking. Many developments since the armistice give it especial point. How can these trade rivalries and other causes of international ill-health be prevented from precipitating an even greater calamity than that through which he lived? The proposed Walter Hines Page School of International Relations, with an endowment of $1,000,000, will seek the answer to this question. It will conduct elaborate studies in the field of international economics, communications, law, racial psychology, geography, diplomatic practice, and other subjects that closely concern war and peace. In years to come this school will thus accumulate a vast fund of information that should help the spread of that international good fellowship and democratic progress to which Page had proposed to devote his last years.

Great Britain has also paid tribute to the man who believed that in acting as her friend and the friend of the Allied cause he was best serving his own country and the world. Soon after the publication of the Page biography, the following letter, signed by the Prime Minister of Great Britain, three former Prime Ministers, and a former Secretary of State for Foreign Affairs appeared in the London *Times:*

Sir:

The publication of the two admirably edited volumes of "The Life and Letters of Walter H. Page" has revealed to the world a personality and a record of achievement of which perhaps only those who came into intimate social and official contact with him during the term of his Ambassadorship in this country were already aware.

In these "Letters" Mr. Page lives again. They give the clearest and widest expression we can ever now hope to receive of his vivid, free-ranging mind and of that mellow integrity of character and abounding humanity which endeared him to us all. More particularly, they show him to have been one of the best friends that Great Britain ever had, and a far-seeing and practical crusader in the cause of Anglo-American coöperation.

In the difficult period of the war, before the United States had entered it, and when many contentious issues inevitably arose between the British and American Governments, it was Mr. Page's handling of these issues, as much as any other factor, that kept them within the bounds of reason and good temper. Scrupulous, as an Ambassador should be, in presenting his country's case with all the vigour and persuasiveness at his command,

Mr. Page's conduct of the negotiations entrusted to him was informed throughout by his native courtesy, humour, and straightforwardness; by a quick understanding of the nature of the European struggle; and by an intensity of sympathy for the Allied cause and of admiration for Great Britain's part in it which was irrepressible. He was the happiest, the most liberated, man in Europe when America entered the war.

For all that Mr. Page contributed toward that supreme development, by smoothing away friction and minimizing and removing difficulties and misunderstandings, this country, no less than his own, owes him an inestimable debt. There must, moreover, be many hundreds of our people who used his services and those of his most efficient staff to inquire after the fate of relatives at the fronts, and who drew freely and gratefully on his exhaustless stock of sympathy, patience, and promptitude.

There is nothing in Great Britain to mark the fact that Mr. Page lived here for five years as United States Ambassador, and that in a great crisis he served his own country and ours, and civilization itself, with a noble competence. We desire to repair that omission. We confidently invite subscriptions to perpetuate a name and services that can never be thought of, on either side of the Atlantic, without deep affection and gratitude.

We are, Sir, &c.,

A. BONAR LAW
BALFOUR
H. H. ASQUITH
D. LLOYD GEORGE
GREY OF FALLODON

The response from all classes of British life was immediate. The opinion was unanimous that there was only one place in Great Britain for a memorial to Page: that was Westminster Abbey. On July 3, 1923, a gathering which completely filled the ancient structure attended services in memory of the Ambassador. A few minutes before this service, Mrs. Walter H. Page, the Ambassador's widow, and other members of the Page family, gathered with the Prime Minister, Mr. Stanley Baldwin, Mr. H. H. Asquith, Mr. Winston Churchill, Lord Lansdowne, and others, in the Chapter House of the Abbey, to unveil a marble tablet in Page's honour. The following remarks were made by Lord Grey:

The tablet that is to be unveiled to-day is in memory of one whose every word and act in great place were inspired by single-minded and earnest desire to make human freedom, as he saw it realized in democracy, prevail among the nations of the world. Walter Hines Page was an example of the truth that the strongest personalities are the outcome not so much of striving for personal success or fame, as of patriotism and of faith in an ideal. His patriotism was of the noblest kind; he loved his country both for what it was and for what he believed it could and would do for the benefit of mankind. His perception of the power of the United States, his belief in its democracy, his absolute and never-faltering trust in the will of its people to do great things and good things for the world, were part of his very being.

Surely it must be a proud as well as a happy thought for his country to remember that it inspired a faith so high in a mind so keen and pure.

I have spoken first of Walter Hines Page as an American because that is how, I am sure, he would have wished us to speak of him and to think of him; but it was very near his heart that there should be between his country and ours true knowledge and understanding each of the other; and there is no greater consummation to be wished for in public affairs than that the high and beneficial hopes for the world which he founded upon this should be realized.

We in this country feel deep gratitude to him; we wish that there should be something to commemorate the sympathy and moral support that he gave us in the greatest crisis of our history. We wish his name to be remembered with regard, with honour, and with affection, as that of one who gave us invaluable help at a time when our liberty, our very independence even, seemed to be at stake.

His countrymen who still cherish the names of those who helped the United States years ago in time of trial and peril will find it easy to understand what we here now feel for such men as Walter Hines Page. In all conversations with him I felt—what I am sure many others here, who knew him, also felt—that there was between him and us a peculiarly close tie of personal sympathy. We felt attached to him by a sense of the same values in public life, by a desire for the same sort of world in which to live, by a kinship of thought, of standards, and of ideals. Therefore, while his resting-place is in his own country, which he loved so devotedly, we have wished to have a memorial here to do honour to him and to preserve for those who come after us a record and memory of his life. It is most fitting that the place for this should be Westminster Abbey—where so much that is great, and honourable, and dear in our history is consecrated—this Abbey, which not so very long ago, as time is reckoned in the life of nations, was as much part of the inheritance of his ancestors as of our own. In this spirit I unveil the memorial and ask the Dean to accept it.

Lord Grey then unveiled the tablet, which bears the following inscription:

TO THE GLORY OF GOD
AND IN MEMORY OF
WALTER HINES PAGE
1855–1918

AMBASSADOR
OF THE UNITED STATES
OF AMERICA TO THE
COURT OF ST. JAMES'S
1913–1918

The Friend of Britain in Her
Sorest Need.

THE END

INDEX TO VOLUME III

1913–1914, 24–25; Prime Minister, December, 1916, 309; Page's estimate of, 312; on separation of Austria from Germany, 367, 370, 373; signer of letter proposing a memorial to Walter H. Page, 428

Lodge, Senator, offers resolution inquiring as to veracity of Zimmermann telegram, 347

London, Bishop of, receives visit of nurses at St. Paul's, 376

Lusitania, torpedoed May 7, 1915, 238; Page's telegram to Wilson as to effect of torpedoing of, 238–240; Page's telegram concerning tragedy of, received by President Wilson less than twenty-four hours after, 240

Maine, Sir Henry, "a lawyer with a style," 11

Mather, Sir William, representative of conservative Englishmen, 249

Mayo, Admiral, his proposed visit to England is cordially approved, 385; receives much attention, 389

McAdoo, Secretary, discussion of financial crisis by, 396, 397, 403

Merry del Val, Spanish Ambassador, calls on Page, 267

Mersey, Lord, 103

Mexico, Wilson's policy, 26–29; English attitude regarding, 35; Wilson's ambition to create constitutional system in, 92; Wilson's "idealism" regarding, 105; murder of Benton in, 106; Benton episode in, discussed by Page and Sir Edward Grey, 109–110; Huerta's downfall indicated, 113; Villa and Zapata regarded as scourges in England, 114; Mexican situation surrendered to South American Ambassadors, 117; flight of Huerta from, 121; Page congratulates Wilson on Mexican conditions, 122; Mexican-Japanese alliance, 342

Monroe Doctrine would be destroyed by Prussian militarism, 139

Moore, George G., Ambassador Page lunches with, 167

Morgan, J. P., and Company's advances to the British Government, 392

Morley, Lord, on our Mexican policy, 35

Navy League, Page speaks at, 103

Newspapers, false impressions given by, 61

No-alliance policy, wisdom of, 130

Northcliffe, Lord, Page visits his country house, 62; says "wisdom" is Ambassador Page's most striking quality, 174; his visit to America criticized, 334; his papers all fair to the United States, 385

Page, Ralph W., opinion of Court "show," 57

Page, Thomas Nelson, Ambassador to Italy, 303

Page, Walter Hines, a careful and careless correspondent, 1; first meeting of Page and Wilson, literary and political interests basis of their friendship, 2; discovers Wilson as a writer, 3; famous for his editorial letters, 4; letter to Wilson requesting articles for *Atlantic Monthly*, 5; letter to Wilson asking for review of Cleveland's career, 7; letter to Wilson on practicability of publishing edition of Bagehot, 9; his admiration for Rooseveltian democracy, approval of Wilson as Democratic candidate, 12; letter to Wilson on Harvey incident, 14; on Wilson's characteristics as a man and a President, 15–16; letter to Wilson regarding study of the Philippines, 17; letter to David F. Houston expressing confidence in the new Administration, 1913, 18; Ambassadorship to England offered by Wilson, 18; arrival in England, May, 1913, 21; influence of American conceptions, 21; his outlook on caste, luxury, 22; his admiration for English standards, 23; his criticism of Jefferson, 23; his sympathy with Lloyd George, 25; picture of English aristocracy, 26; views on changes in Church and State, 26; question of primogeniture and entail and vital social and political changes in prewar period, 26; his agreement with Emerson on real strength of British nobility, 27; report to the President of interview with King George, 30; lecture at Royal Institution on "Some Aspects of the American Democracy," 31; his attitude toward royalty, 31, 32; letter to Wilson concerning Central and South America, 33; opinions on British aristocracy, 36, 40, 41; speaks at Shakespearean celebration, 42; speech on Shakespeare at Stratford an expression of his attitude toward all great literature, 44; letter to Wilson on gaiety of London season, 46; informal comments of aristocratic ladies on war situation, 49; court presentations described, 51; notes on the English Revolution, 59; passing of Panama Canal Bill triumph for Wilson and Page, 60; his distress at perverted newspaper reports, 61; visits Lord Northcliffe at his country house, 62; repeal of Tolls clause general topic, 64; congratulates Wilson on success of his Mexican programme, Carden's influence less, 65; writes Wilson on English hospitality as a fine art, 66; House adjourns because Mr. Asquith is dining with the American Ambassador, 67; special envoys besiege the Ambassador, 69; need for adequate salary for official expenses of Ambassador, 73; his friendship with Sir Edward Grey, 78; states need of increase of salary and describes duties of Ambassador, 79–80; change of living conditions makes $50,000 necessary, 83; writes letter to Wilson

In praise of Irwin Laughlin's services to the Embassy, 87; explains phrase "English-led and English-ruled" to President Wilson, 89; warm personal relations with Wilson, 92; shocked and saddened by European conditions, 93; writes Wilson proposing official visit to London, 96; speaks at Authors' Club on "President Wilson as a Man of Letters," 97; mentions Wilson's son-in-law and daughter on their honeymoon in England, 100; designates Sir Edward Grey, "the biggest Englishman I have met," 108; reports to Wilson effect of Benton's murder in Mexico, 109; suggests advisability of prompt cables on Cabinet meetings, 110; explains baseball game to King George, 110; emphasizes influence of King George's personality, 111; believes Wilson's opposition to Huerta was salvation of parts of Central and South America, 112; writes Wilson of predictions of Huerta's downfall, 113; his consolatory advice to English banker on Mexican situation, 115; writes Wilson enthusiastically of Colonel House, 117; on college relations and political feeling, 118; Ambassador's reception, 120; Royal Literary Fund Dinner, Page's speech at, misunderstood in newspaper reports, 121; anecdotes of proffered sale of Panama Canal, 121; congratulates President Wilson on Huerta's flight, 122; writes of interview with Sir Edward Grey in regard to using good offices of American Government in war issues, 125; description of Grey as man and statesman, 126; war inevitable, why not now and have it over, 129; "while writing, news comes of Germany's declaration of war against Russia and her marching into Luxembourg," 129; England cut off from Continent, 130; American shipping and foreign commerce to gain, 130; Wilson's Administration probably made historic by war, 130; Page sends letter of condolence to Wilson, 131; his early efforts for social reorganization in the South, 133; describes difficulties of situation in first days of war, 135, 136; his confidence in Sir Edward Grey, 136; outlines conditions that made war inevitable between Germany and England, 137; says England will reject any terms from Germany save on basis of defeat, 141; no escape from subject of war, 145; London muffled, 143; his recollections of Germans as a boy, 145; account of English ladies and their work, 146; reports of peace meetings in the United States, 146; no end to changes war will bring, 147; most important figures in the diplomatic situation, 152; his policy clear and consistent, 154; his frankness with Sir Edward Grey, 156;

the question of American ammunition being sent to England, 157; comments on Kitchener's directness and "cheek," 158; receives many letters concerning America's attitude, 160; runs soup kitchens, 160; war essentially between England and Germany, 162; unprecedented fierceness, 164; possible death of civilization to follow "clash of systems," 165; message from General French, 168–169; telegraphs Bryan of conference with Sir Edward Grey about possible mediation, 170; believed the United States could end the war, 171; on reduction of armaments and restriction of military authority, 172; outlines formula to Wilson, 174, 175; on Declaration of London, 176, 180; has conference with Sir Edward Grey, 177; protests against Lansing's despatch on Declaration of London, 181–188; threat to resign, 188; writes Wilson of immediate effect of American withdrawal of demand that England accept the Declaration of London, 189; the tight rope of neutrality, 193; "French would have probably collapsed but for Belgian check of Germans and English help," 194; feeling that Russians may suddenly quit, 194; reports lying rumours everywhere, 195; requested to give personal aid on all sides, 196; says world after war will thank God for United States, 197; Christmas letter to Wilson, 1914, 198; sees suspicion of German influence in the United States, 199; arranges for Colonel Squier to go to front in France, 205; sends telegram to Secretary of State concerning Colonel Squier's visit to front, 208; reports to Wilson of Squier's visit and its result, 209; a silent war, 210; reports interview with General French to Secretary of State, 212; comments on international reporting of President Wilson's speeches, 213; writes Wilson of Belgian refugees, 216; is kept in ignorance of situation in Washington, 220; Foreign Office and its attitude toward American Ambassador, 221; his suggestion that *Dacia* be seized by French Navy, 222; outlines public opinion in England, 227, 228; has talk with Sir Edward Grey on German merchant ships, 229; economic pressure in forcing German merchant ships off the seas, 230, 231; his handling of *Dacia* crisis prevented war between the United States and England, 237; his telegram to Wilson on effect of sinking of *Lusitania*, 238–239; telegraphs Wilson of English criticism of lack of action by United States on *Gulflight* and *Lusitania* cases, 242; expresses satisfaction on Wilson's first *Lusitania* note, 245; his further report on English opinion, 248; writes Wilson that English impression is that "peace at any